CREATIVE GARDENING
with Dermot O'Neill

Good gardening

Dermot O'Neill

GILL AND MACMILLAN
and
RADIO TELEFÍS ÉIREANN

Published by
Gill and Macmillan Ltd
Goldenbridge
Dublin 8
and
Radio Telefís Éireann
Donnybrook
Dublin 4
© Dermot O'Neill 1990
0 7171 1813 4
Edited by Roberta Reeners
Designed by Design Image, Dublin
Colour photography by John Cooney
Colour origination by Kulor Centre Ltd
Printed by Criterion Press, Dublin

CONTENTS

To Maura and Peter, my parents, and my grandmother, Hanora Hall, who patiently guided and encouraged my love of plants and gardens and all growing things.

INTRODUCTION

A friend recently remarked that moving house caused him few problems, but leaving his garden was too much to bear. I understood immediately. He was articulating a personal attachment so many people feel. To them, the garden is a place of refuge from the hectic modern world, an escape back into some earthly Eden.

Gardens assume an importance due to the human effort and endeavour of their owners. A rose bed, new trees, special shrubs or the humble vegetable patch offer possibilities for beauty and utility. Moreover, increasing numbers also see gardening as their chief leisure activity. In such circumstances, there is more experimenting and the word 'creative' often crops up. Believed to be the exclusive preserve of writers, artists and fashion designers (who often resort to the garden for inspiration), I firmly believe that gardening too merits such a creative label. Indeed there is historical evidence to substantiate this claim.

Two definitive examples of creative gardeners were the Victorian, Gertrude Jekyll, and her Irish-born contemporary, William Robinson. These two people did most to shape modern gardening through their writing and application. By putting the emphasis on things like colour and perspective, Jekyll and Robinson created a new role for the gardener. The evolution of gardening also benefited from early twentieth century plant hunters who brought back specimens from such diverse locations as the Andean rain forests and the slopes of the Himalayas. Meanwhile, hybridisers were busy experimenting and the fruits of their labours were extremely important for future gardeners. Thanks to the mixture of new ideas and new plants, there were all sorts of opportunities to create colourful, not to mention fruitful, gardens. Similarly there was a blending of styles. For instance, European/American garden designs were influenced by Japanese traditions.

A far cry, this, from the stuffy gardens of Victorians who surrounded their villas with miniature 'Alpine' effects, displays of ferns and winding tiled paths. Yet the changes went further. Gardening gained a universal appeal which was hard to match. So much so that now, whether children of eight or pensioners of eighty, the garden brings joy to everyone. Whether the garden of a stately home or a small suburban plot, creative potential is all around. Even people who have owned gardens for years and have never given them much thought - beyond periodically and reluctantly mowing the lawn - realise the possibilities. All that is best from the past has been combined with a constant thrust of new ideas and plants to preoccupy the modern gardener.

The influence of creative gardening is best seen in a typical garden. Though there is no average gardener (approaches and traits vary quite considerably from person to person), consider Green Fingers as a representative model.

In times past, Green Fingers would have been quite happy to allocate front and back into two-thirds lawn, leaving the rest for flowers, shrubs or vegetables. The emphasis was on formal arrangement, with rectangles and squares imperative. Flowers were paraded out in military fashion, with rose bed displays akin to a Red Army parade. Old Green Fingers thought little about colour co-ordination. Garden features were limited to a gnome. Garden tools were used when the need arose - before they were cast aside covered in mud and rust. The lawnmower (circa 1945) still gave a good cut with one blade.

One day in the garden centre while searching for a new gnome, Green Fingers came across a book on creative gardening. Words like 'informal, perspective, colour co-ordination, lawncare, bonsai, dwarf shrub, water gardens' leapt from the pages. Suddenly, a whole new world of gardening opened up.

Neighbours once walked by Green Fingers' garden without a thought. Now they stop and marvel. Not only are the flower and shrub arrangements stunning, but the lawn always has a healthy appearance, even when every other garden is burned to a frazzle. Perhaps the subtle seasonal colour changes are the key to the attraction. Others maintain that it is the pond plants and fountain which set this garden apart. Green Fingers has no time to admire right now. The implements require cleaning, the mower servicing, and plans are afoot for a new greenhouse and conservatory. Then there is planting and pruning, not to mention a trip to the garden centre for a honey locust tree.

Creative gardening is nothing if not a continuous activity. Leaving the garden to fend for itself or resting on past laurels does not produce results. Always mindful of how to use mechanical aids in the garden, the creative gardener effectively incorporates propagating beds, ventilators or shading blinds. Similarly, such a gardener sees the value of keeping a compost heap and the correct use of weed killers or fungicides. Even the matter of soil composition is treated with proper respect.

Energy, as Green Fingers knows, must be matched with perception and imagination. The creative gardener keeps abreast of trends, but sees through gimmicks. Yet, what really counts is accumulated experience with plants and soil. There is no substitute for trial and error in plant management. Above all, a creative gardener must learn to proceed at nature's pace rather than human haste.

Those people who enjoy RTE's 'Live at 3' gardening spot will derive further satisfaction from this book. At the same time, I hope anyone new to creative gardening will find a wealth of information and helpful hints to guide them on their way.

✿ ✿ ✿ ✿

1. ASSESSING THE GARDEN

It is often said that there are horses for courses - and so it is with plants and gardens. Before galloping into the garden with a new plant, I always reflect on whether or not it will be suited to its new environs. Natural garden conditions and/or manmade features so often conspire against a creative idea. Those who supply us with plants and seeds today will tell us that we have aids available of which our forebears never dreamed!

✿ ✿ ✿ ✿
Soil Composition

Uppermost in a gardener's mind is soil composition. Soil may not sound the most interesting of topics - indeed it rates very low in the creative gardening stakes too. However, creative gardeners, in common with many others, need some knowledge of soil in order to get the best from whatever they plant. Flowers are choosy about where they live, and more particularly about what sort of soil they will grow in. Camellia do best in acid soil, for example, but wallflowers positively detest it. Knowing such information helps when it comes to planning flower borders.

Some will say, fair enough, don't plant wallflowers in acid soil. But detecting acid in soil is not a matter of looking down at the ground for a big 'A'. Nor does acid confine itself to one type of soil. Light, heavy and especially clay soil can contain acid since it occurs due to a deficiency of lime. The degree of acidity or alkalinity will influence what can be grown. In a lime-rich soil, the rhododendron tribe will never be happy and hydrangeas will be pink rather than blue. Slight

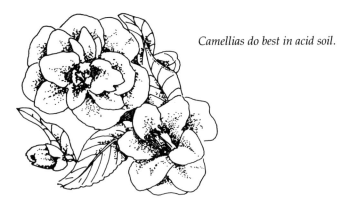

Camellias do best in acid soil.

acidity suits the majority of garden plants, while the inclusion of peat, organic matter from compost heaps, animal manure and acidic fertilisers will all ameliorate excess alkalinity.

Garden centres have special testing kits for measuring soil acidity. Using the pH level of the soil as a measurement, gardeners can calculate whether an area is suitable for certain plants. Any reading below 7.0 means the soil is acid. Therefore degrees may vary from 6.5 (slight acidity) to anything below 6.0 (heavy acid concentration). Most plants will find it difficult to survive in soil below 6.0. Taking soil from one patch of ground distorts the overall acid content. To get an accurate reading, it is important to collect soil from several well-spaced points. Mixed together, the samples give the acid count. One tangible sign of high acidity levels is an abundance of moss on the lawn, but only a very low pH level would cause this.

Various substances affect acidity levels in the soil. Peat and sulphate of ammonia increase acid levels. Gardeners can combat high levels of acidity by using dressings of ground limestone. This works by breaking down clay soil and will have a prolonged effect.

Gardeners with acid soil conditions need not despair. There are numerous plants which thrive without lime or which will tolerate a good degree of acidity. Among the lime-haters, azaleas, camellias and heathers are popular choices. Shamrock ericaceous compost (without lime), rainwater (tap water is often too limey) and a large container are provisions required for the aforementioned plants. With proper drainage at the base of the container and with regular feedings with Miracid, the plants will do fine.

Several trees tolerate high levels of acidity including *Eyceyphia*, *Halesia* and *Picea*. In the bulbs category, lilies are the most predominant lime-haters. *Lilium auratum*, *Lilium rubellum* and *Lilium tigrinum* grow well in an acid soil. Other shrubs suitable for acid soils are: *Clethra*, *Fothergilla*, *Gaultheria*, *Halesia*, *Kalmia*, *Magnolia* and *Vaccinium* (bilberry, blueberry and cranberry). Heathers like callunas and ericas thrive in acid soils, but will grow elsewhere too.

✿✿✿✿
Drainage

Drainage can be quite a problem in the garden. Some gardens hold a lot of moisture, and it is sometimes necessary to take drastic steps. Introducing drainage pipes should be undertaken before you start levelling the garden.

Proper drainage may seem a big problem at first. Both plants and people need air and water to survive, but they need them in the right amounts. Most plants need a soil which is moist, but well drained. Very few plants can survive with their roots constantly in water. At the same time, any soil that is water-logged is also a soil from which air is excluded, and plants need air at the roots to live.

A more practical solution to a drainage problem is to adapt to prevailing conditions. Simply plant specimens which are suited to moist soil. *Cornus* (Dogwood) and rhododendrons are two shrubs which like the wet. Lobelia and primula are two perennials suited to similar conditions. There are also a number of annuals and bulbs which are partial to damp soil.

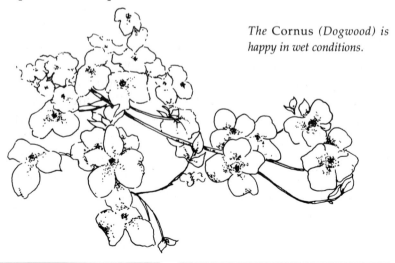

The Cornus *(Dogwood) is happy in wet conditions.*

Lack of sun frequently thwarts the creative touch, but this is to ignore quite a number of flowers which prefer shade. Choose from *Aconitum* (Monkshood), *Myosotis* (Forget-me-not) or *Lunaria* (Honesty) if partial shade exists. *Viola* (Pansy) and *Convallaria* (Lily of the valley) are among the flowers which tolerate dense shade.

The success or failure of any plant will depend to a very large degree upon the thoroughness with which the soil has been prepared. But just as important is correct planting. In general, however, there are two important rules: plants should always be planted firmly, and should always be planted to the correct depth.

❀ ❀ ❀ ❀
Get Rid of the Weeds

One thing all gardens need, especially the more fertile, is a good weeding. There is no excuse for allowing weeds to overrun the garden when there are now so many ways to get rid of them. A strong, complete weedkiller will kill everything for about six to nine months. Complete weedkillers for large areas are simple to use and generally effective. They are watered on with an ordinary watering can or one with a dispensing bar. Land treated with sodium chlorate in the early autumn and dug later in the year after the weed-killer has taken effect will be ready for sowing the following spring. It is not so simple where weeds are growing among shrubs and flowers. Here, use foliar weedkillers such as ICI Weedol.

When using weedkillers, one must be very, very careful and follow instructions on the packet or bottle. I cannot stress this enough! Be careful that the weedkiller does not come in contact with the foliage, as some weedkillers are absorbed by the leaves and kill the very plants one wants to grow. Annual weeds and those spread by seed can easily be discouraged with a draw hoe. Rhizomatous and other types of perennial weeds such as nettles require a special preparation for dealing with them. Selective weedkillers are useful for killing brushwood or weeds in rough grass and should be used in dilute form for this purpose according to the instructions. Weeds with runners overground, like the creeping buttercup, should be dug out or be treated with ICI Weedol. Lawns are cleared of weeds by various types of selective weedkillers or lawn sand.

✿✿✿✿
Additional Features

While the mundane tasks are hardly inclined to excite creative gardeners, they do at least provide the opportunity to assess design details. Generally speaking, beauty is in the eye of the beholder, something most gardeners would find hard to disagree with. I find more people turning away from the manicured lawn and rectangular flower bed towards more informal arrangements. An individual garden design is good to see, but again it is best combined with a practical approach.

An extraordinary number of gardeners locate sheds for tools or compost heaps in remote corners. Far better to place these facilities where they can be reached without difficulty, keeping them screened with a climber-covered trellis. In this way the work load is cut, and creative credibility remains intact.

Patios offer endless opportunities for creating a bridge between the house and the garden. Yet sometimes the degree of shade from the house has a detrimental effect on patio pot plants. In this instance, aim for a sunny spot with good access. Plants will benefit and a less formal patio will result.

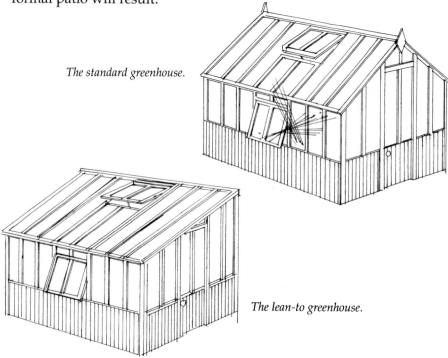

The standard greenhouse.

The lean-to greenhouse.

Gardens paths are more likely to be chosen with design rather than use in mind. Some end up looking like an accidental boreen, too narrow to carry barrowloads of fertiliser or peat. Paths should be bold, perhaps 4 feet (+1m) in width, and slightly above ground level. This type of path is both useful for transport and a recognisable garden feature.

Contrary to a volume of opinion, the greenhouse is not an extension of the garden shed. Hidden away in a dark area, the greenhouse cannot give plants what they want: heat and light. Bring the greenhouse out into the open, giving it an artistic shape by incorporating domes or other extensions. The building serves its purpose and also adds to a garden's attraction.

The true mark of a creative gardener is a person who can somehow make the ugly seem attractive. Barriers and fences are a case in point. A combination of a low fence and a flowering hedge just above is a touch which enhances a bare wall or fence.

A thing of beauty is a joy forever. Certainly this applies to the garden. Thought and imagination go a long way to ensuring that garden features will enhance the image and please the admirer.

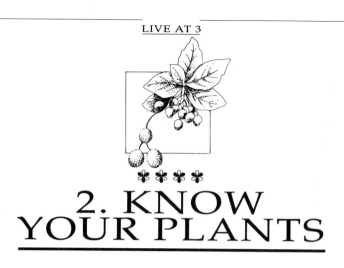

2. KNOW YOUR PLANTS

Creative gardening would mean very little were it not for flowers. Colour in the garden throughout the year need not be a mere dream. By careful planning it really is possible to have something in bloom or to capture the attention, whatever the season or weather.

The choice of flowers determines the overall impression in the garden. Knowing how to choose plants is therefore very important and should be thought out well in advance. Shrubs are the main providers of winter flowers. Even among the herbaceous plants, the Christmas and Lenten roses provide interest from Christmas onwards. Throughout the summer there is no shortage of colourful plants. The problem is more one of harmonising the various elements of the garden.

✿✿✿ *Categories of Flowers*

According to some garden centre proprietors, many people cannot distinguish between different categories of flowers. When presented with the choice between half-hardy annuals and herbaceous perennials, the first-time gardener may often register a blank look. Yet there is little mystery attached to these words and summary knowledge of the main flower groups can help enormously in making the right choice for the garden.

Try and balance your garden so that the interest is not all in one section while another area is bare. Plant spring bulbs among the herbaceous plants. Grow ground cover plants with attractive foliage between shrubs to hold interest when they are not in flower. To keep interest in the rockery, plant small summer and autumn-flowering bulbs. These will create colourful areas after the main flush of spring colour.

Perhaps the most uncomplicated range of plants around are the bulbs (buds growing beneath the surface). Take daffodils and tulips. Left to their own devices, bulbs for both these flowers will produce masses of red and yellow each and every spring. Some bulbs like *Gladiolus* give flowers in summer, while others such as some crocuses turn up in autumn. Most remarkable of all is *Cyclamen coum* which shows a white or pink flower in winter.

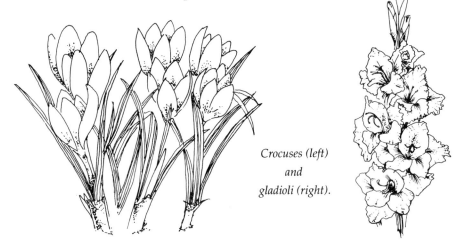

Crocuses (left)
and
gladioli (right).

'Herbaceous perennials' sounds like a grandiose title, yet these plants require only moderate attention from the gardener to survive over several years. These are plants which flower in the summer, die down in the autumn and reappear the following spring. Perennials will live for an indefinite period. Herbaceous plants form a permanent source of colour and interest in the garden. They are bold plants, capable of seeing out a bad winter. The plants take a year or two to become established and flower well. They will then come up every year with little attention, other than weeding or maybe dividing a large clump. They are at their best when planted in borders with shrubs. Poppies, hollyhocks and sunflowers offer some of the most remarkable shapes and summer colours among herbaceous perennials. (For more about herbaceous perennials see Chapter 12.)

✣ ✣ ✣ ✣
Bulbs, Corms and Tubers

The category of flower referred to as tubers get their name from enlarged roots which act as a larder during winter. These underground storehouses, with their varied and brightly coloured flowers, seldom fail to please. Below soil level, tuber stems bear buds for next year's flowers. All this might imply that tubers are well able to look after themselves. Quite the contrary - they need special care. Begonias, for instance, require glasshouse cover for the duration of autumn and winter cold spells. Dahlias are another form of tuberous plant which need to be lifted each autumn.

Bulbs, corms and tubers are often all classed as 'bulbs' but this is not so. Bulbs, corms, tubers and rhizomes are all quite different in their construction and appearance, and can be readily identified.

Bulbs : A true bulb is formed of layers of modified leaves which surround the embryo shoot in the centre of the bulb. The rings of modified leaves can be seen if a bulb is cut in half cross-wise. An onion would be a very good example of a bulb. Daffodils, hyacinths and tulips are also bulbs.

Bulblets produced by the parent bulb.

Corms : A corm is really a thickened stem. When cut in half cross-wise it appears solid, unlike the layers to be found in a bulb. The thin, papery scales found on the outside of a corm serve as protection only and do not have any food reserve. A very good example of this are gladioli.

Tubers : These are thickened or swollen underground stems or roots. Just like bulbs, they are able to store food. The dahlia is a good example of a root tuber as it does not bear buds. Potatoes are stem tubers, and they bear buds. These can be seen as eyes which can produce stems and leaves.

Rhizomes : These are stems found partly above and partly below the soil. They can be fast growing such as couch grass, or fast and slow growing as with bearded irises. Rhizomes act as storage organs.

Bulbs may be used for forcing to help decorate the home during the winter and spring. They are also useful as seasonal bedding plants which are lifted after flowering, or as permanent plantings in the open ground, such as under trees and shrubs.

❀❀❀❀
Rock Plants

There is something of a contradiction about rock plants. That elegant and delicate flowers such as *Armeria* (Thrift) manage to survive in a seemingly hostile environment of rock is itself a miracle. An explanation may come with the other name given to rock plants - Alpines. Remember these little plants started life in crevices high in the mountains above France and Switzerland. They are hardly likely to be intimidated down among the rocks of suburbia. They do not appreciate wet areas, but thrive in carefully-prepared conditions with or without rocks. Rock plants come in all forms and are a bright addition to the garden.

❀❀❀❀
Annuals and Biennials

'All too brief' might be a phrase applied to annuals. Going through their full cycle in only a season means that these plants will die after flowering. Biennials take two seasons to complete flowering but, like annuals, die afterwards.

For sheer colour, annuals and biennials are difficult to beat. The annuals in particular provide as near 'instant' gardening as one can expect. The backbone of summer bedding is formed by the half-hardy (frost-tender) annual, while the hardy types can be sown and grown where they are to flower with the minimum of preparation or fuss. They are also very useful for filling in spaces among herbaceous plants or shrubs. If growing your own annuals or biennials from seed, try sowing seed earlier or later than normal. It is then possible to extend the flowering season. Many annuals and biennials are F1 varieties, with extra and more uniform vigour, but seed saved from them will not produce the same results, so I would always buy fresh seed each year.

Annuals and Biennials for Partial Shade
Ageratum
Begonia
Bellis perennis (Double daisy)
Coreopsis (Calliopsis)
Cynoglossum (Hound's tongue)
Digitalis (Foxglove)
Impatiens (Busy lizzie)
Mimulus (Monkey flower)
Myosotis (Forget-me-not)
Oenothera biennis (Evening primrose)
Primula polyantha (Polyanthus)
Verbascum (Mullein)

Annuals and Biennials for Sunny Spots and Borders
Alyssum maritimum
Arctotis
Bartonia aurea (*Mentzelia lindleyi*)
Cosmea (Cosmos)
Eschscholzia Californica (Californian poppy)
Annual gaillardia (Blanket flower)
Iberis umbellata (Candytuft)
Papaver rhoeas (Field poppy)
Salvia (annual type)
Tropaeolum majus (Nasturtium)

Digitalis *(Foxglove).*

❀❀❀❀
Climbers and Container Plants

The ability of climbers to decorate any unattractive barrier or garden surround can test a gardener's creative potential to the full. Climbers are extremely useful not only for their colour but also for their speed of growth. Many varieties are available, but chief on the list is the fragrant sweet pea. Nasturtiums deserve a mention because of their universal popularity. Both plants flower during the summer. Sweet peas came in various shades of lilac, pink, white and red, with nasturtiums coloured blood red through to shades of peach, apricot and yellow.

Although there are many perennials suitable for window boxes, troughs, tubs or any container, it is the annuals that provide the real body of colour. They look pretty from outside the house and have the merit of bringing the outside into the home. By intensive planting they can provide colour and interest at all seasons. Troughs, tubs and other containers should not only be considered for the town garden or patio. Tubs and other containers can be moved around to create a changing scene. They also make it possible to grow plants with special soil requirements.

Most of the annuals planted in containers are half-hardy, which means that they have to be raised in heat, but they can all be bought in May or June as bedding plants. Whenever possible, buy pot-grown plants and use Shamrock multipurpose compost in the container. Because the plants are in a confined area, be prepared to feed once a fortnight during the summer, using a liquid fertiliser.

When planting your window box, always use fresh compost. Ensure that the drainage holes are clear and line it with a layer of broken crock or small stones. Then fill it with your Shamrock multipurpose compost and start planting.

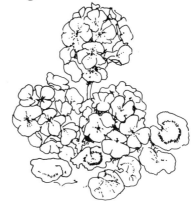

Good Container Plants
Ageratum
Begonia
Lobelia
Nemesia
Petunia
Tagetes
Pansy
Pelargonium

Pelargoniums are excellent container plants.

These are some plants that look well in a container and will give beautiful colour all summer.

❀ ❀ ❀ ❀

3. TOOLS OF THE TRADE

❀ ❀ ❀ ❀
Spades, Forks and Hoes

It is often said that it is a bad workman who blames his tools. When it comes to gardening, every job has the right tool. Without the right tool, even an easy job can be backbreaking.

Good tools are not cheap, but the list of basic gardening equipment is not vast, and you can add the more expensive refinements later. A good brand name to look for is True Temper — Irish-made in Co. Cork.

Having spent good money on tools, it is very important to look after them. The humble spade is a case in point, since it seldom fully gets the recognition it deserves. Too often, the gardener claims full credit for creative efforts without once considering the razor-sharp blade. Once work is completed, the razor-sharp spade is cast aside in the garden shed. Amateur gardeners do not seem to realise that looking after garden implements is just as important as gardening. Cleaning and oiling tools before putting them away in a dry place prevents rust and keeps them sharp.

Proper care can also make a gardener's life easier. Take a simple example. Dry soil left on a spade gathers more soil next time it is used. Images of weekend (not to mention weakened) gardeners spring vividly to mind as they struggle purposefully with a spade caked up with one hundred weight of surplus soil! If they survive digging like this, our intrepid workers should consider Olympic weightlifting next time round.

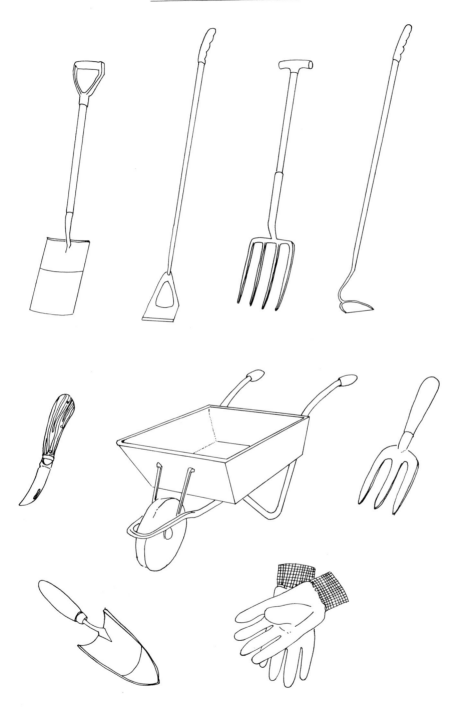

A variety of garden tools.

Consider the tools and think of each one as a friend. The spade is a trusty mate if smooth, bright and sharp at the blade. Spend money on a good spade, but buy well. Blade lengths vary from 7-12 inches (18-20cm), and different types are designed for different strengths of use.

Some spades, forks and hoes are made with chromium-plated or stainless steel blades. These are not only less sticky to use but also less likely to damage from rust and corrosion, although they are more expensive.

Forks are garden chums for life and are very undemanding in terms of attention. They come in all sizes, the most useful being the sturdy four-pronged type for heavy digging and the light border fork for older people's use or for working in borders crowded with plants. The fork is very handy for shallow cultivation around permanent plants like roses and herbaceous perennials. It is rarely misused unless a novice tries to dig with it.

The hoe is a most popular type of tool for weeding around young plants or breaking up the soil around them. There are a few varieties of hoe - the Dutch hoe or its cousin the Paxton hoe. They all operate on the chopping principle and incorporate a fairly narrow blade positioned at an angle to the handle. Hoes may also be used to make seed drills. The traditional Dutch hoe has a D-shaped blade and is worked with a push-pull action to loosen the soil and slice heads off annual weeds.

A rake, unlike its human namesake, is a refined character. It should not be used with a heavy hand, but rather with a delicate touch for levelling ground for grass sowing. If handled like a bludgeon, the rake will take up valuable soil with surface weeds, while leaving unwanted debris behind semi-hidden. The standard metal-tined rake with up to fourteen stout teeth is most useful to help break down the soil after working it with the back of a fork. It is also useful for working in fertiliser. The rake is also used for making seed drills and covering the seed.

❋❋❋❋
Hand Tools and Sprayers

Two more faithful servants are the hand trowel and fork. They come into their own in rock gardens and borders, as well as for potting and greenhouse culture. Trowels can be bought in various sizes and are useful for digging out bulbs and small plants. They can be used to make small planting holes. (A pointed stick called a dibber is also used for this job.)

Hand forks are often used for mixing small amounts of compost in the greenhouse and for cultivating pot plants. You will keep these tools for years if you clean them of clay and dirt after each use.

Sprayers are useful for distributing insecticides, weedkillers and foliar feeds. For most needs, a hand pump supplying one gallon or half-gallon is all that is needed. Reasonably-priced pressure pumps are available, including the knapsack types which are more convenient to use.

❀ ❀ ❀ ❀
Shears and Secateurs

Finally a mention for the terrible twins - the shears and the secateurs. When you buy these tools, buy good ones first time round and look after them. These tools need a lot of pampering to keep them in tip-top shape for working among hedges and tight corners or pruning trees and shrubs. Putting an edge on cutting tools and keeping the temper of the hardened metal demands a degree of skill. It is important to sharpen only the top levelled surface. Under no circumstances rub where the blades intersect. To do this would be to destroy the blade association and impair the cut.

❀ ❀ ❀ ❀
The Dynamics of Digging

The skilled gardener will know most about looking after garden equipment and can also use each piece of equipment most effectively. Digging is a case in point. Few people understand the dynamics of digging and most regard it as a backbreaking chore. There are a number of essentials to remember. First, dig a trench at least a foot (30cm) wide. This will stop freshly-dug soil from falling back on upturned ground. Secondly, dig down to the full depth of the spade face, sliding the lifting hand down the shaft. Then, lever the top of the spade with the other hand and gently lift the earth up.

To demonstrate how to use an implement it is worth considering the hoe. A tall person will probably hold a Dutch hoe underhand, a shorter person might decide to use an overhand grip (the shaft pointing straight or over the shoulder). Someone of medium height could use the hoe both ways. There is value in versatility. No strain is put on individual muscles. The hoe works quickly up and down rows and finally the gardener can manoeuvre about awkward places without changing stance.

Buying garden tools requires a certain common sense. No less than golf clubs, it is worth sticking to brand leaders as they are often the most dependable. Garden centres, hardware shops and DIY stores all stock Irish-made True Temper and many other leading brand names.

The garden tool works best for the gardener who chooses carefully, uses it effectively and cleans/stores the implement carefully after use.

❊ ❊ ❊ ❊

4. COLOUR IN THE GARDEN

❊ ❊ ❊ ❊
The Nature of Colour

There is a popular myth in some gardening circles which goes something like this - Bright is right, green is humble. This is a stock response to the general trend towards garden colour at any cost. Such a trend is modern, with little or no precedent in the history of gardening. Right back to Renaissance times, gardens were valued in terms of design, shape, light and shade. Colour for colour's sake was apparently not an issue. I believe it has contributed little to creative gardening. The creative gardener should know how to use colour effectively. By implication this involves becoming acquainted with the nature of colour in plants.

Colour is reflected light altered by surface pigments. Plants have two major pigment types – carotenoids and anthocyanins. Carotenoid is responsible for yellow and its variations - yellow roses, orange carrots. Anthocyanins bring out all other colours in the spectrum, such as 'geranium red' and 'delphinium blue'.

While pigments play the major role in determining colour, things like proteins and acids can also affect the tone of the plant. For example, hydrangeas will turn blue if acid is present, but pink or red in an alkaline soil. They are, in effect, like litmus paper.

However some of the most important influences on plant colour, as far as the creative gardener is concerned, come from light itself. Plants respond to different degrees of light. And light, in turn, is affected by latitude, humidity and temperature. Plants in Ireland therefore tend to lack the contrasting colours of, say, southern Spain.

The effects of light on plants are clearly visible during summer months. On a particularly hot, sunny day, pastel shades will have a distinctly bleached look, while the more intense colours like red absorb the sun's rays. At night, the reds will fade completely, while the pastels come into their own, shining brightly because of their pigmentation. All this is worth bearing in mind when deciding on which colours to choose. In this instance, 'all bright' would clearly not be 'all right'. Far better to make a judicious plant selection based on a knowledge of colour.

❀ ❀ ❀ ❀
Colour: Contrast and Harmony

While picking wallpaper or paint presents a few minor headaches, it is nothing compared to choosing plant colour schemes! Sometimes, a gardener may be powerless to prevent a nightmare in technicolour since nature has a habit of upsetting the best laid plans. For example, retarded flowering times may result in a whole break up of planned colour co-ordination. Conversely, an early flower can clash with the general garden tone.

Too often, however, colour problems with plants can be put down to the gardener - or, more particularly, a gardener's poor memory. Like incandescent flames, colourful summer flowers fade faster from a poor memory than from a sudden drop in temperature. Thus, unsuitable flower colours are juxtaposed the following year and much tearing of hair occurs. By contrast, a creative gardener is alive to such possibilities and benefits from hindsight. Learning from experience is one way to avoid pitfalls; checking colour cards is another. A gardener no less than an artist needs to know a few words from the language of colour.

'Complementary' colours mean maximum contrast – red and green for example, 'Primary' colours (red, yellow and blue) when mixed together produce all other shades. Translating this information into gardening terms, flowers of yellow and flowers of blue split fairly evenly along the divide on the spectrum between red and green. This means flowers approximating to yellow look better grouped together. Similarly, various shades of blue are at ease in the same bed. Even with this simple information, the creative gardener can arrange for contrast and harmony.

When aiming for contrast in plant colour, the gardener is encouraged to go to extremes. 'A riot' of colour with the whole gamut of hues (a hue is the actual place on the spectrum, such as magenta) presents an exciting scene. Complementary colours look best when well matched, as in small clusters. The result is a bold fight for supremacy, pleasing to the eye. On the other hand, closely related tones (a tone is the quantity of pigment in a flower) tend to merge their differences in hue to achieve an understanding. Woodland browns and greens appear harmonious when 'muddied' to the same degree. As a general rule of thumb, try to keep colours like yellow-pink and blue-pink apart. These colours are neither brave enough to carry the contrast nor suitably subdued to blend.

�**✿✿✿✿**
A Single Colour

Creative gardening should always make a a good impact. One way to get a positive response is through a single colour array. Masses of one colour or variants of the same may reflect a gardener's single-minded personality. Yet, if successful, single colours do most to create a mood garden.

Dominant and popular, white gives the gardener a great range of flowers from which to choose. White honesty, veronicas, cyclamen, and clematis - not to mention roses, campanulas, daisies and daffodils - give some idea of the multitudes on offer. Skilled gardeners use white to create the setting. A central arbour of climbing white roses over an iron frame provides the perfect canopy for a garden with several hedges.

If white is compatible, red is not. True, red flowers or leaves disguise bulky spaces and may offer strange and rich effects. There are, however, several difficulties with the colour. Except for tulips, almost no early flowers come to prominence. Secondly, red borders in a green setting depend very much on light. In good light, reds are welcoming; in bad they shy away.

From dark to bright – and no better colour than yellow to cheer the mood. Gold borders and flowers are not in short supply, but should not be overdone. Tone down a loud yellow border with a pervasive blue. Alternatively, raise the volume slightly (if required) by adding in a reddish flower like chrysanthemum.

Silver-grey foliage turns quite a few heads but such plants are not noted for their flowers. Blue does not lend itself to mass exposure because there are so few varieties of flower in this colour. Going up the spectrum to pale purple tints, it is possible to develop ideas in lavender, lilac and violet. Green is a difficult colour to emphasise for obvious reasons. But it does at least focus attention on the composition of the plant.

Single colour gardens are arresting spectacles. They also mark a return to classical examples, with a heightened role for light and space. Single colour provides the gardener with an excellent opportunity to develop creative approaches.

❀ ❀ ❀ ❀
More Tactics with Colour

Arranging garden colour is rather like trying to conduct an orchestra. One wrong move and the whole symphony goes out of tune. In gardening terms, such an occurrence might be reflected in a 'riot' of colour.

The seasons call the tune when it comes to colours. Winter's quiet tones show up in a selection of sophisticated shades. Spring offers a lively melody of complementary colours. Summer's serenade of green sets off the more ostentatious blooms. Finally, a crescendo in beauty is reached with autumn's dramatic entrance, with leaves turning colour.

The creative gardener, while allowing for seasonal adjustments, still holds the conductor's baton. Integrating diverse elements of colour is not an easy task. But it can be achieved with due attention to certain rules.

Contrast as a central theme is unlikely to work. In isolation, colour contrast may create the desired effect. This is especially true with red and green. Careful control of dark leaf colours, bushes and shrubs can govern bright flowers, especially reds or yellows.

Red and blue colours can appear to alter the dimensions of the garden. There is a scientific explanation behind this phenomenon. The eye finds it more difficult to focus on red than on other colours. Sudden eye contact with a patch of red flowers distorts any composed view in the garden. Distance is brought closer unless there are compatible red flowers planted in gradual progression. Blue poses few focus problems for the eye. As a colour, it tends to fade into the background. Used with a contrasting colour, a bank of blue flowers creates an impression of distance. This is particularly useful in a small garden, giving depth where there is little.

Effective use of contrast depends on two key considerations. First, lighter colours benefit from a wider space among plants with stronger tones. Secondly, when using strong contrast (such as introducing a brilliant flower), pave the way with an intermediate colour. Among the latter range, white and grey prove most useful because they rarely clash with anything around them.

To get the most out of colour, exploit light. Beds of flowers look most striking when planted to the south and west. In these positions, the sun provides the necessary illumination to show plants in their best light.

Plants adapt to the surrounding light, sometimes with surprising results. A clearing among the rhododendrons provides the ideal spot for planting some bright flowers (pale tulips within a group of forget-me-nots). The illusion created is one of sunlight breaking shadows. This example illustrates better than most the potential of colour and light.

5. A TREE FOR EVERY GARDEN

'O dreamy, gloomy, friendly trees.'
Herbert Trench

❀ ❀ ❀ ❀
Choosing the Tree

Since trees so transform a garden and the moods therein, it is extremely important to consider this point before planting one. The creative aspect of gardening depends on overall effect. If a tall tree is the pivotal point in a small garden, it can render borders and beds insignificant. On the other hand, a number of small trees, combined with shrubs, can provide cover and shelter as well as a perfect background to set off other garden features.

While much depends on the size of the garden, there are certain aspects of tree growing common to any location. First and foremost is the choice between deciduous and evergreen. Deciduous trees offer the dramatic moments in a garden, with their seasonal costume change. Evergreens have a title role, often setting the perfect scene for everything else. Seasonal colour is worth a mention be it foliage, blossom or bark. A tree can determine the prevailing atmosphere of the garden, whether autumn excesses, spring fever or summer subtlety. Creative gardeners always try to incorporate trees into a general picture.

Practical judgment is also required in tree choice. A spreading chestnut tree might sound romantic, but gardeners like other mortals have only so much time available. Exceptions aside, the tree may look like a bonsai when first purchased but could grow to a height and spread way beyond acceptable bounds. How impressed will neighbours be by an arboreal Berlin Wall?

Trees are somewhat selfish when it comes to light, so features such as water gardens may suffer as a result. Likewise, soil quality under trees is poor, though narcissi and crocus bulbs may not complain when they get leading parts to play here.

Assess the effect of a tree on the house. Remember that long winter shadows can shorten daylight hours considerably. Tree roots have little respect for manmade drains and house foundations - a point worth enforcing when it comes to the question of site.

A trip to the local park might give some ideas about selection and suitability. Later, when picking an outlet from which to purchase a tree, it is worth going to some specialist nurseries. While ordinary garden centres keep a fair variety of species, specialist suppliers are more likely to have better choices and more rare trees. This might be the case with young, small trees which do well in an average garden. These trees are a popular choice since they become established after a couple of years.

Nurseries and garden centres present their trees in a number of ways. Deciduous varieties are usually in the ground and lifted when purchased. Evergreens are grown either in containers or with a supply of soil wrapped in plastic. Container-grown trees, including evergreens, are always in something more substantial than loose sacking. Bare-rooted trees should have many fibrous roots, with good shoots and stem.

❋ ❋ ❋ ❋
Planting the Tree

Before buying a tree, check its soil preference. No less than other garden plants, trees look for particular soil conditions. Though a species might survive in less than ideal soil, proper cultivation before planting is essential. Uncultivated soil might contain stumps or roots of old trees which have been infected by the deadly honey fungus. Such soil is unsuitable for new trees.

By contrast, digging loosens the earth, allowing roots a good supply of humus and plant nutrients. Cultivation also extends to subsoil. This maintains a drainage system which is so vital to the growth of tree roots. To get at the subsoil, dig a hole 12in(30cm) deep and separate soil at the bottom of the hole. The previously removed topsoil acts as a base for the special planting mixture which should also contain strong compost and bonemeal. The ground is now ready for planting.

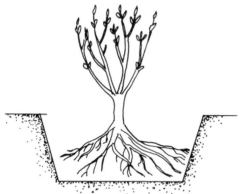

Plant the tree in the hole up to the soil mark on the stem.

Work some planting mixture around the roots.

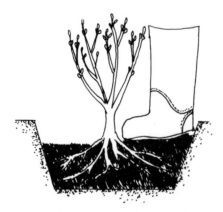

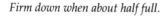

Firm down when about half full.

A shallow ring around the planting hole forms a water-retaining basin.

Planting a tree.

▲ *Pink, red and yellow tulips create a springtime symphony of colour.*

▲ *The elegant lily will grace any border.*

▲ *A splendid show of tulips and grape hyacinth* (Muscari).

▲ *A well-designed rock garden.*

▲ *The* Mimulus *or monkey flower is suitable for borders and rock gardens.*

▲ *Mellow brickwork is enhanced by a window box display.*

▲ *Annual poppies suit even the smallest garden.*

▲ *An example of perfect colour harmony.*

▲ *Golden grass and day lilies* (Hemerocallis) *- perfect complements.*

▲ *A blue border juxtaposed with silvery-green foliage.*

▲ *The simple perfection of green and white.*

▲ *The maple Acer griseum - grown for its beautiful bark and outstanding autumn colour.*

▲ *The Japanese maple -* Acer palmatum *- with purple and green foliage.*

▲ Garrya elliptica - *a shrub grown for its attractive catkins.*

▲ *The glorious gold of the rose 'Graham Thomas'.*

▲ *A bold display of dwarf tulips.*

Plant the tree in the hole up to soil mark on the stem. A stick placed horizontally across the hole will verify when the soil mark is at ground level. It may be necessary to add or remove subsoil in order to achieve a level measure. Secure a 5ft(1.5m) stake close to the centre of the hole. Now begin to fill it with the prepared planting mixture. The enriched soil should go over and between the roots. Firm the soil occasionally with a boot until the hole is filled. In dry conditions, soak the ground after planting.

To finish, fasten the tree to its stake with an adjustable strap (available from most garden centres). This helps support the tree in windy conditions, while at the same time allowing the roots to take proper hold. A word of warning though - make sure the tree stem is not touching the stake, as this will damage the back.

✿ ✿ ✿ ✿
When to Plant

Trees have different preferred planting times. With heavy soil, mid spring is most suitable for evergreens (autumn is not out of the question, providing the soil is more refined). Deciduous trees ought to be planted in their dormant period – between autumn and the start of spring. Container-grown trees of any kind do not have special planting times, but freezing or sodden conditions should be avoided.

Of the many trees to choose from, I have divided the selection here into types specifically for small gardens and those suitable for larger sites.

Trees for small gardens

(D= Deciduous; E= Evergreen)

◆   *Acer palmatum* 'Dissectum' (D)
     (Japanese maple)   Grows up to 10ft(3m), with similar spread. Colourful and shrub-like. Best seen in autumn.

◆   *Crataegus oxyacanthoides* (D)
     (Hawthorn)   A height of 15ft(4.5m) is its maximum, with a spread of similar proportions. The tree's haws are scarlet. Before these, white, pink or red flowers appear, depending on the form of hawthorn. In addition to sun, it also appreciates light shade.

◆ *Cryptomeria japonica* 'Elegans Nana' (D)
(Japanese Cedar)   Height and spread of only 3ft(1m) make it a very small cedar. Sun.

◆ *Gleditsia triacanthos* (D)
(Honey Locust)   Average height of 15ft(4.5m), a spread of 12ft(3.5m). Delightful display of yellow leaves in autumn. Sun.

◆ *Juniperus virginiana* 'Sky Rocket' (E)
(Juniper)   As the name suggests, a slender tree at only 2ft(60cm) spread with a height of 12ft(3.5m). Useful colour with its grey leaves. This conifer takes light shade and sun.

◆ *Laburnum anagyroides* (D)
With a height of 15ft(4.5m) and a spread of 12ft(3.5m), there is much to admire about its yellow flowers in June. Choose from the weeping or upright varieties. Sun.

◆ *Malus* (D)
(Crab apple)   Goes to 15ft(4.5m), spreads 12ft(3.5m). Several types to choose from in this range, including *Malus floribunda* and *Malus* 'Red Sentinel'. The former has white flowers and yellow fruit, the latter red fruit. Sun, light shade.

Trees for moderate-sized gardens

(usually take a good few years' growth)

◆ *Acer griseum* (D)
(Maple)   A tall tree at 40ft(12m) and a spread half its height. Notable for its orange trunk colour when bark is peeled back. Foliage colour in autumn is spectacular. Slow growth. Open position. Any soil.

◆ *Acer negundo* 'Variegatum' (D)
(Box Elder)   Grows to 20ft(6m) with a 15ft(4.5m) spread. Tends to spread outwards, with white-edged leaves. Open position. Any soil.

◆ *Arbutus unedo* (E)
(Strawberry tree)   Slow in reaching its 20ft(6m) height and 15ft(4.5m) spread. This tree combines a gnarled appearance with white flowers and strawberry-like fruits. Likes shelter and warm temperatures, but grows in any soil.

◆ *Betula papyrifera* (D)

(Paper birch)   Big tree - 50ft(15m) high with 20ft(6m) spread. White bark, yellow leaves and graceful habit make this tree stand out. Suited to any position and soil.

◆ *Cercis siliquastrum* (D)

(Judas tree)   Hardly an appropriate name for this pretty 15ft(4.5m) high, 12ft(3.5m) spread tree. Interesting leaf shape combines with small, rosy flowers in spring, followed by long seedpods. Likes sun and shelter, with any soil.

◆ *Davidia involucrata* (D)

(Pocket-handkerchief tree)   A height of 20ft(6m) and a spread of 15ft(4.5m). Its name gives a clue to the shape and colour of petal bracts. However, trees must be ten or more years to achieve this appearance. All soils and position.

◆ *Eucalyptus niphophila* (E)

Good-sized tree at 30ft(9m) with a 15ft(4.5m) spread. Bark features grey, cream and green colours when flaking. Long leaves account for its evergreen status. White summer flowers make this a most attractive tree. It is fussy about conditions, wanting a well-drained, moisture-retentive soil. Likes a lot of sun and full shelter from cold winds.

◆ *Ginkgo biloba* (D)

(Maidenhair tree)   At a height of 40ft(12m) and spread to 15ft(4.5m), this tree produces spectacular yellow fan leaves in autumn. Adaptable to soil, but needs sun and shelter.

◆ *Pyrus salicifolia* 'Pendula' (D)

(Weeping pear)   Is 15ft(4.5m) at full height, with a total spread of 10ft(3m). Soft and graceful is the theme, from its willowy leaves to its weeping habit. Creamy spring flowers contribute to its attractiveness, but fruits are for eating. Open position. Any soil.

◆ *Robina pseudoacacia* (D)

(False acacia)   30ft(9m) high with a 15ft(4.5m) spread. True blend of foliage, fragrance and flowers (early summer) are the hallmarks of this tree. Grows in any position and soil. 'Frisia' produces yellow-golden flowers.

◆ *Sorbus* 'Joseph Rock' (D)
(Rowan/Mountain ash)   Reaches 15ft(4.5m) high and 10ft(3m) spread. Outstanding autumn leaf colours. Creamy flowers in spring and yellow fruits for autumn make it a most useful tree. Added values are its adaptability to any soil and situation.

◆ *Thuja plicata* 'Zebrina' (E)
(Western red cedar)   Up to 30ft(9m) high, but a small spread of about 8ft(2.5m). A conical habit combines with regular cedar foliage, highlighted by bands of creamy yellow. This is a slow-growing tree which prefers sun and well-drained soil.

❀❀❀❀
6. DWARF SHRUBS

❀❀❀❀
An Interesting Compromise

Very small gardens do not lend themselves to large flowering and evergreen shrubs. Thwarted by space, the gardener frequently finds it difficult to control colonies of large shrubs as they set up outposts all over. Restrictions on light and air mean other plant inhabitants are smothered by these marauders.

Gardeners never intend to ignite a battle for survival in the beds and bushes, but the lure of shrubs often proves irresistible. Dwarf shrubs provide an interesting compromise for creative gardeners who want to combine small bushes or trees with flowers. Shrubs in this class grow to about 4ft(1m) (half that among herbaceous varieties) so they are by no means true miniatures.

Thankfully, collecting dwarf shrubs is not an expensive hobby. Local garden centres stock a wide range. Judicious selection from some shrubs mentioned here will enhance any small garden.

❀❀❀❀
Springtime Choices

My favourites are the dwarf Prunuses. In April, shades of pink flowers characterise *Prunus tenella.* Included here, 'Dwarf Russian Almond' contributes to a spring of perestroika in the garden with its bright pink colours. Also setting exciting tones is 'Fire Hill', with deeper shades of pink. Dwarf Prunuses are really in the pink, and *Prunus triloba* is no exception, offering double flowers all along its branches. This shrub requires shoot pruning immediately after flowering.

Cushioning the colourful impact of the Prunuses, dwarf willows have a small but subtle presence. Soft grey down covers *Salix helvetica's* young stems, leaves and catkins, making it a most attractive foliage plant. The gentle *S. lanata* is a woolly willow with silver-tinged leaves. It grows to about 3 ft(1m) and is definitely worthy of inclusion.

Spireas are attractive summer shrubs.

✾✾✾✾
Summertime Shrubs

Tardiness is not usually an attribute welcomed in the plant world, but dwarf forms of Spireas are exceptional shrubs. Some, like *S. thunbergii's* chaste white flowers come out in June. Others transform the garden mood at a time when shrubs are not noted for displays. The revolutionary flowering patterns are packaged in attractive colours. Coming into their own in late summer are *S. bullata*, a Japanese variety with rose-crimson flowers, and *S. albiflora*, a splendid white bloom to provide balance. Hybrid varieties flower from June to September. *S. x bumalda* along with *S.* 'Anthony Waterer' (both hybrids from *S. japonica* and *S. albiflora*) give deep pink and crimson flowers respectively.

Dwarf Viburnums ring changes in autumn, with *V. davidii* one of the most popular due to its turquoise-blue fruits. Grow two or three in a group to guarantee fertilisation.

Another plant to include in autumn plans is the deciduous species of the Berberis (Barberry). Standing at 4ft(+1m), *B. thunbergii* makes no attempt to camouflage its spectacular foliage and scarlet berries. Racemes of rose pink flowers on *Indigofera gerardiana* arrive late in the year, yet this leguminous shrub must be rated as a live candidate for any garden.

✿ ✿ ✿ ✿
Further Choices

Dwarf shrubs are given adopted homelands for a variety of reasons. An example is *Acer palmatum* 'Dissectum' (Japanese maple), popular in the smallest gardens. Extreme slow growth stops the plant encroaching on others. *Acer palmatum* 'Dissectum Atropurpurem' wins over hearts with its deep red leaves in autumn. Reliable and unobtrusive, Daphnes are first choice with a lot of gardeners, the white *D. mezereum* combining well with the purple-red *A. mezerum*. The latter is not strictly a dwarf, but is a very tidy plant all the same. Original blue blooms are a striking characteristic of *Ceratostigma willmottianum*, while *Philadelphus microphyllus* has a pineapple scent to accompany single white flowers. *P. manteau d'hermine* is probably the most dwarf Philadelphus.

Competition for living space in the garden may be fierce, but dwarf shrubs solve more problems than they cause. Consider *Betula nana*, the 4ft(+1m) birch tree. It retains the slender lines of the original birch but can grow in very small gardens. This plant, along with others like *Cytisus kewensis*, the dwarf broom, gives gardeners options they would not normally have. Adding in Rhododendrons, Azaleas and all lime-free soil plants, the list of dwarf shrubs to choose from is vast.

✿ ✿ ✿ ✿
Slow-Growing Dwarf Conifers

◆ *Abies balsamea* 'Hudsonia'
(Silver fir) This grows to 2ft(60cm) with a spread of 30in(75cm). Note its compact form and aromatic fragrance. Suited to any soil and position.

◆ *Chamaecyparis lawsonia* 'Minima Aurea'
(Lawson cypress) With a full height of 3ft(1m) and spread to 30in(75cm), this tree gives bright yellow foliage to accompany its conical shape. Takes any soil and situation.

◆ *Juniperus communis* 'Compressa'
(Common juniper) 36in(90cm) tall with a 1ft(30cm) spread. A grey-green foliage colour and columnar habit are its chief features. Grows in almost all places and soil types.

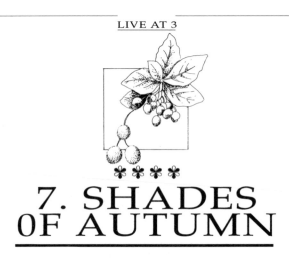

✤ ✤ ✤ ✤

7. SHADES OF AUTUMN

✤ ✤ ✤ ✤
Many Opportunities

Autumn colour is often underestimated and unplanned. One year, while reflecting on my own garden during 'the Fall' (an appropriate Americanism perhaps), I came to the conclusion that it could do with more colourful plants to emphasise the season's beauty. It seemed that leaving autumnal colour to chance was to ignore a vast range of trees and shrubs which look their best at precisely that time of the year.

Small is the watchword for trees in town gardens. Yet compact trees can have sophisticated colour coverings in autumn. Look no further than *Prunus sargentii* - 'Sergeants cherry'. Not much bigger than a bush, it follows a blush-pink flower in spring with an outstanding autumn tint which is hard to compare.

An abundance of white flowers in April, small edible red-to-black fruits in June are the costume changes which Juneberry *Amelanchier canadensis* completes before settling on crimson to end the year.

Shrubs offer unlimited potential for creativity in autumn. A case in point are the Barberries. Their spectacular heart of gold in late spring is matched by the attractive autumn berries and the glorious leaves on deciduous varieties of the shrub.

The Barberry is exceptional, but it does highlight the colourful effects which you can arrange for autumn in the garden. There is a whole range of shrubs to choose from. Azaleas, hardy deciduous plants, are tailored for growth in confined areas. They change in a kaleidoscope of colour as the seasons progress. The shrub's beautiful flower and light green foliage of summer give way to alternating gold and scarlet in autumn. Similar to the Azalea (in its preference for lime-free, peaty soil), but less common, is *Enkiathus campanulatus.* It is a shrub with bell-shaped cream-yellow flowers in May, producing golden-reddish tints as the year draws to a close.

Rosa moyesii *produces striking hips in autumn.*

Roses and Shrubs

No less striking in autumn are the Rose species with their exotic 'hips'. *Rosa rugosa* and *R. moyesii* are prime examples with their predominant red fruits. Well worthy of consideration in autumnal plans is Virgnia creeper, *Ampelopsis,* which paints a rouge canvas on walls. Forget any worries about damaged brickwork or damp. Unlike ivy, this creeper climbs on small sucker pads with no penetrating powers beyond the surface. Nor does *Ampelopsis* accommodate insects, since it is deciduous and does not develop matted growth.

Among deciduous shrubs to go out in a blaze of autumn colour are *Euonymus alatus,* with its unusual wing stem, and *E. europaeus.* The latter, known as the spindle tree, is quite big. Changes in its leaves are combined with shining orange fruit, split open to declare red seeds. Enjoy the colour, but watch out for the predatory blackfly which the species attracts.

Sophisticated shrubs and trees add lustre. However, gardens also demand evergreens to tone down the denuding effects of the later seasons on deciduous plants. An interesting evergreen like *Arbutus unedo*, the strawberry tree, is just the mask for an area deprived of foliage. A large bush (10-15ft/3-4.5m) of different guises, it also provides suitable variation in the garden. Pitcher-shaped white flowers characterise its first autumn appearance, followed by bright red fruits the subsequent autumn. The strawberry-type flesh ripens with a succeeding yield of flowers.

❀ ❀ ❀ ❀
A Hint of Grey

Grey leaves enhance the garden, sprinkling a different colour across autumn's hues. Lavender, Santolina and dwarf silver and golden conifers fall into this alternative range. Caution is urged with variegated forms of shrubs as they are sometimes 'spotty'. *Euonymus radicans* and *E. japonicus* deserve a place in the picture, the former for its cheerfulness, the latter for colour co-ordination.

Autumn and winter provide a challenge to the gardener. In dull conditions, colour offers relief. Impressions created depend upon the choice of trees and shrubs. There are many to choose from, apart from those mentioned.

8. FLOWERING SHRUBS: TEN OF THE BEST

Gardeners have never had such a wide choice in flowering shrubs. Now, creative ambition need not be confined to high summer. The selection available is such that even the owner of a moderate-sized garden can have something in bloom all year round. I usually plan my selection of shrubs by the fireside on cold afternoons (for once a spot of armchair gardening can be justified!). After deliberation, the following ten shrubs always appear on my shopping list. They are among the most popular in garden centres or nurseries.

◆ ***Arbutus unedo***

The strawberry tree is one of the finest of all evergreens and hardier than is generally supposed. Beautiful in winter when its panicles of urn-shaped white blossoms appear, the shrub more than matches this effect in autumn when hung with strawberry-like crimson fruits. This is one of the few ericaceous shrubs that will tolerate lime.

Another handsome species is *A. menziesii* with its blend of colours. Large, glossy-green leaves vie for prominence with rich terracotta bark, while the pyramidal panicles of white flowers are followed by orange fruits.

A good loamy soil with plenty of humus, freely drained, will suit both. There is no need for pruning.

◆ *Berberis* (flowering evergreen)

The Berberis is an invaluable plant, especially *B. darwinii*. A range of colours adds to its worth. Flames, crimson and orange, rich golden yellow, and gold are selected forms. The dwarf and hybrid forms also contribute to its variety. Among the latter, *stenophylla* is exceptional. A large bush with long sweeping branches gilded with orange blossoms, it rivals *darwinii* in splendour and general merit. There are a number of dwarf shrubs similar to *stenophylla.* Among the best is the 4-6ft(1-2m) *corallina* with coral-red and orange flowers.

◆ *Ceanothus* (evergreen)

These delicate blue-flowered shrubs still manage to winter safely against a wall in all but the coldest localities. Well established are the bright blue *C. dentatus, apillosus, veitchianus,* and the early violet-blue *rigidus* which has a fine variety grandifolius. Competition is provided by a crop of new hybrids such as 'Delight', 'Autumnal blue' and the powder-blue 'Buckwoodii'. The latter is an ideal choice for the creative gardener. It is 3-4ft(c.1m) high and a late bloomer. Other hybrids grow 6-10ft(2-3m) or more.

Favourite conditions for these shrubs are a light, stony soil with full sun. Shorten back-flowering ends as blooms go off.

◆ *Choisya ternata*

Also known as Mexican orange, this is a hardy and useful evergreen. Its chief characteristics are aromatic trefoil leaves – corymbs of 1-1·5ins(30cm) - and white fragrant blossoms. A second blossom yield often occurs in autumn. *Choisya ternata* grows to about 7ft(2m), with a wide spread. Best situated in a loose soil and sunny position, but comes on almost anywhere, even under trees.

◆ *Escallonia*

Quite a substantial grouping, it includes evergreen and deciduous shrubs which are dwarf, medium and large. While the evergreens are best suited to coastal gardens, some can survive anywhere. 'C.F. Ball' is a prime example, as are 'Slieve Donard' and *Edinensis macrantha* with its pink rosy-red flower. *Iveyi* provides a good contrast with its white blooms.

Among the non-evergreen types, top choice is *Langleyensis*, with whiplash branches wreathed in carmine rose flowers. The majority listed are summer bloomers which are not fussy about soil or placing.

◆ *Garrya elliptica*

A seaside dweller, this tough Californian evergreen is primarily ornamental. The large bush bears a cluster of emerald-grey and yellow drooping catkins in mid winter. Male *Garrya elliptica* is especially impressive, since its catkins often grow 10-15ins(25-40cms) long. Prefers to exist in poor soil.

◆ *Mahonia*

Has returned to a genus of its own after a stay among the berberis. The old *M. aquifolium* is worthy of regard, with clusters of lemon-yellow (March-May) and blue-purple fruits. Appearing in many forms, it serves well as a carpet of undergrowth in sparse woodland areas or under individual trees. *M. bealii* is a superior example, with large leaves and bold flowers of lemon-yellow fragrance which bloom in spring. Of equal merit is *M. japonica,* quite similar in colour to *bealii,* though its racemes are less vertical. *M. nepalensi* is another good sort, though not as hardy as *bealii.* Striking and reliable, it rates high among this class.

All Mahonias can be cut down to near ground (during spring) when leggy.

◆ *Spartium junceum*

This remarkable shrub, know as Spanish broom, is one of the finest around. Not only is it easy to raise from seed, but will also flourish in any light soil. Fragrant clusters of 'golden sweet peas' appear from June to September. In spring, flowering twigs may be shortened or the plant clipped over to present a formal shrub. *Spartium junceum* should be liberally grouped or planted at the back of the shrub border. Height ranges from 5-10ft(1.5-3m).

◆ *Ulex europaeus fl. pl.*

The double gorse is at its best when the perfumed yellow flowers cover its heavy trusses. Other qualities which set this shrub apart include a long-lasting flower (compared to common gorse), a compact shape and a short height.

Thriving on hot, arid slopes with full sun, the double gorse proves the ideal companion for heather. There is no difficulty in raising this shrub from cuttings.

Double gorse.

◆ *Viburnum* (deciduous)

There are many beautiful viburnums from which to choose. *V. bitchiuense* gives a fragrant flesh-pink flower in late summer. *Carlesii*, at a height of 3-4ft(+1m), is a special shrub. Its rosy-white flowers offer a delightful scent in springtime.

Fragrans, by contrast, flowers in winter. Colours range from pale pink to white and it grows 5-6ft(2m). *Grandiflorum*, a large vivid rose, (larger in flower than *Fragrans*) is very sensitive to frost.

The popular snowball tree has several varieties but *Opulus* stands out. *Tomentosum plicateum*, otherwise known as the Japanese snowball tree, is a refined shrub. *V.t. Mariesii* has a distinguished round shape and grows to a height of 6-8ft(2-2.5m). Fishbone branches laden on the top side with cream-white flowers (bracta) make this an extremely attractive lawn shrub at the height of summer.

Viburnums require no special garden conditions. Propagate from cuttings, rooted off-sets. No pruning needed.

9. ROSES

Undoubtedly the most popular flower, the rose enjoys an immortal place in every gardener's heart. Among poets in particular, roses have an acutely symbolic presence. Witness these lines by Kisa'i of Merv:

> 'Roses are a gift of price,
> Sent to us from paradise,
> More divine our nature grows,
> In the eden of the Rose.'

Symbol of perfection, beauty, love or whatever, roses offer continuity and fragance, combined with impeccable bloom and foliage. As a gardener, I think these qualities elevate the rose to an exalted level. Whether planted in massed borders or given a solitary position, the flower retains a unique prominence.

Five Classes

There are five classes from which to choose. *Hybrid tea roses* get first preference in most popular polls, not least for their big flowers and firm buds.

Floribundas rate inferior to hybrid teas in terms of flower (clustered at the ends of branches), but make up the difference in reliability and endurance.

Miniature roses attract a lot of attention on a novelty level, with a wide range available. Miniatures are a definite pretender to the title of most popular rose.

Climbers and *ramblers* have loyal followings. Climbers are useful to cover walls and fences. Their large blooms often give a repeat flowering. Ramblers bear all their small flowers on one-year-old wood and therefore should be cut down to soil level every autumn. This type of rose has the added advantage of being very easy to grow.

Finally, the *shrub roses* are enjoying a belated surge towards favouritism, thanks to the choice of old-fashioned varieties which come under this heading. Plants in this category are sometimes quite large and flower throughout the summer months.

With so many to choose from, gardeners go down different rose avenues. However, beginners might consider hybrid teas, floribundas and climbers the most suitable. On displays of flower (hybrids in the back garden, floribundas in the front) and versatility (climbers will go up house walls, garden fences, even old apple trees) these classes give great value.

❋❋❋❋
Starting a Rose Bed

Planting and pruning of roses demands extra attention. For this reason I have given these areas special mention in the next chapter. Here, the emphasis will be on planning, preparation and after-care.

November is the ideal month for starting a rose bed. Plan for uniform effect in colour and height. I recommend a bed for each variety of rose, as the effect *en masse* is far more spectacular than a mixed array. In choosing a place for rose beds, pick a sunny yet sheltered area in full view of living room windows. Roses are not troubled by soil, but they are bothered by land lying sodden in winter.

In preparation for planting, clear the ground of perennial weeds. Fork lightly over the ground and apply Rose Plus simultaneously. About 4oz(100g) to the square yard (c. square metre) is an adequate amount.

Then consider the distances between each rose plant. Give 20in(50cm) for strong growing hybrid teas; 18in(45cm) for floribundas and dwarf types. Allow 8ft(2.5m) apart for climbers and ramblers.

The next step is to prepare a hole for each rose bush, 15in(40cm) square and 17in(45cm) deep.

Getting roses ready for planting requires similar attention to detail. Check for broken or damaged roots and remove these. The tops should be cut back at least 6-8in(15-20cm), with all but the sturdiest stems removed. Climbers are the exception. Where the bark looks green or not dried out, leave at least two feet.

❀ ❀ ❀ ❀
Tending your Roses

Once planted, roses need cautious tending. To start, cover the bed with medium-grade peat one inch(2.5cm) deep. Wild growths, or suckers as they are called, sometimes come up from the roots. Recognised by very small leaves and extreme prickly stems, suckers should be cut below soil level.

Roses will want food twice a year, in February and July. 4oz(100g) of Rose Plus fertiliser to the square yard will suffice to keep plants satisfied.

Health is not guaranteed by food alone. Three main scourges afflict roses: mildew, black spot and greenfly. Mildew produces a white powder over leaves and stem. Black spot lives up to its name. Stem and leaves get large blotches of black but this disease can be tackled. Greenfly, minute insects which attack undersides of leaves and tips of shoots, are a rose grower's nightmare. Spray with Rose Clear and repeat the dose twice at five day intervals.

The choice of roses is vast, so I have picked personal favourites in each of the classes to compile the following list. These roses are generally available from leading garden centres and nurseries. Use the following as a checklist when selecting roses.

Hybrid Tea	Colour	Scent
(S=slightly fragrant; V=very fragrant)		
Alec's Red	Crimson	S
Ernest H. Morse	Rich crimson	V
Fragrant Cloud	Rich crimson	V
Grandpa Dickson	Lemon yellow	S
Mullard Jubilee	Deep rose-pink	S

Pascali	White	S
Peace	Yellow-edged pink	S
Piccadilly	Red-yellow reverse	S
Red Devil	Scarlet	S
Super Star	Orange vermilion	S
Wendy Cussons	Deep reddish-pink	V
Whisky Mac	Golden apricot	V

Floribunda	Colour	Scent
Allgold	Buttercup yellow	S
Arthur Bell	Golden yellow	V
Elizabeth of Glamis	Orange salmon	V
Evelyn Fison	Vivid scarlet	S
Iceberg	White	S
Pink Parfait	Pink	S
Tip Top	Salmon pink	S

Miniature	Colour	
Baby Darling	Orange pink	
Baby Masquerade	Yellow pink-red	
Cinderella	White-edged pink	
Easter Morning	Ivory white	
Little Buckaroo	Bright red	
Little Flirt	Red-yellow reverse	
New Penny	Red pink	
Starina	Bright vermilion	
Yellow Doll	Soft yellow	

Climbers (C)/Ramblers(R)	Colour	Scent
Albertine R	Pale pink	V
Aloha C	Rose pink	V
Bantry Bay C	Pale rose-pink	S

Danse de Feu C	Orange scarlet	
Dorothy Perkins R	Rose pink	
Emily Gray R	Buff yellow	
Étoile de Hollande C	Deep red	V
Excelsa R	Rosy crimson	
Golden Showers C	Golden yellow	V
Guinée C	Very dark red	V
Handel C	Creamy edged rosy pink	S
Mermaid C	Primrose yellow	S
New Dawn R	Shell pink	S
Schoolgirl C	Apricot orange	S
Swan Lake C	White tinted pink	S
Zéphirine Drouhin	Carmine pink	V

Shrub Roses	Colour	Scent
Blanc Double de Coubert	Pure white	V
Buff Beauty	Pale apricot	V
Fritz Nobis	Salmon pink	V
Frühlinsgold	Creamy yellow	V
Graham Thomas	Yellow	
Maidens Blush	Blush pink	V
Mme. Isaac Pereire	Deep carmine pink	
Nevada	Creamy white	
Roseraie de l'Hay	Wine red	S

10. CARING
FOR YOUR ROSES

'O Rose, thou art sick!
The Invisible worm
That flies in the night
In the howling storm

Has found out thy bed
Of crimson joy;
And this dark secret love
Does thy life destroy.'

Blake's 'The Sick Rose' seems an appropriate introduction to the subjects of planting and pruning, since these two activities are most important in maintaining healthy roses.

Planting

In keeping with her position, the queen of flowers requires a spacious boudoir. Before planting a rose, dig a hole adequately wide and deep to cope with extended roots. In cramped conditions, roots may suffer from drought and eventually suffocate. Let the original soil mark on the rose stem (left over from the garden centre) act as a guide to depth. This mark should never be above ground.

Rose roots require choice soil. Work the rose bush gently up and down as each spadeful of soil is introduced. This induces soil to percolate between fine roots. Once the top roots are covered, firm down by using only the heel of the boot. I like to flood the hole with copious quantities of water after the first firming. Water consolidates soil around the roots (more soil can be added to avoid excess mud). Add a little Shamrock tree and shrub compost. To complete planting, fill the hole, firm and level off.

✿✿✿✿
Pruning

Pruning roses is not about snipping randomly, a practice which will most likely result in rapid deterioration of the plant. Far better to prune with foresight and intelligence. Bear in mind also that different species of roses require different types of pruning. I prefer to prune hybrid teas and floribundas on or around St Patrick's Day. For others, I advocate winter pruning, though a mild season can activate buds long before March is over. Early pruning of active buds causes energetic development among the remainder, with subsequent vulnerability to frost damage.

Hybrid teas and floribundas benefit from balanced pruning. Severe pruning of weaker growths is advised. The result is a reduction to about two buds in frail sections of the plant, and five or six buds in stronger growths.

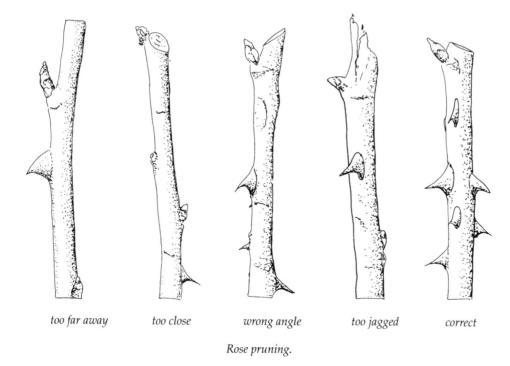

| too far away | too close | wrong angle | too jagged | correct |

Rose pruning.

As a rule of thumb, select an outward-pointing bud as the leading shoot on shortened stems. In a sprawling bush, pick the uppermost bud. Such action helps determine the shape of the bush and prevents inter-crossing shoots in the centre. Check for and remove very weak, old and dead shoots along with any snags. Do this before pruning. Hybrid teas appreciate a more comprehensive pruning than floribundas.

Rambling roses seem by nature carefree and uncomplicated plants. Certainly, pruning of ramblers is relatively straightforward. In most cases, prune after the last flower has faded so retained shoots can ripen before the onset of winter. When pruning, cut growths down from their supports. Fasten the desired amount of young wood and cut the rest down to the base. Retain only the most healthy growths, cutting back all old flowering areas. When young basal shoots surface, tie them in to prevent straggling. Growing points on irregular shoots are open to severe damage.

A rose demanding different treatment is the climber. Very light pruning should take place in spring. Remove dead wood and weak shoots. Every year, sever the oldest shoots right out at the base. This will keep growth strong and encourage substitute growths.

Shrub roses never look for more than a tidy trim in late March to keep cover on the bushes.

Proper planting and pruning will ensure a happy rose which is safe from the elements.

✻ ✻ ✻ ✻
11. BULBS, CORMS AND TUBERS

Bulbs are some of the most valuable plants available to the creative gardener. When few other flowers are out, spring bulbs like tulips, daffodils and narcissi set the scene. Storage possibilities mean they can be lifted from a bed and replaced by plants with more urgent requirements. As miniatures in rock gardens, among biennials or simply in massed beds, bulbs are perfectly at home. Their one dislike is sodden soil, but even this is balanced by the fact that they can grow on uncultivated ground beneath trees.

The generic use of the word 'bulb' can also include corms and tubers since they too have storage organs and root systems below-ground. With a few exceptions (tulips and gladioli), bulbs give annual displays of flowers without much attention from the gardener. Their undemanding nature undoubtedly attracts but is not the only point in their favour. Container bulbs, especially crocuses and dwarf narcissi, find popularity in homes without gardens. Bulbs really are the 'convenience plant' even when it comes to their purchase. Bulb specialists produce detailed catalogues which allow customers to make summer orders.

✻ ✻ ✻ ✻
Planting Bulbs

Planting bulbs presents few problems. Late summer/early autumn is the best time to put bulbs down. Well-drained soil with a good treatment of organic fertiliser and proper weed clearance prepares the ground. Space bulbs according to directions, but try for a random arrangement as the display will be far more lively. Remember, too, single plants will hardly flatter.

Give bulbs good depth, a hole three times their height is the usual measure. Bulb planters are available but a trowel will suffice. Container bulbs are planted later in autumn. Ensure proper drainage (broken pieces of pottery covering the base) before filling container with suitable compost.

❀ ❀ ❀ ❀
Lifting and Storing

When spring and summer flowering takes place, some plants need to be lifted. Container varieties should be taken up before foliage dies down and replanted in another place. In this way, the bulb can build up its reserves while leaving the container free for summer flowers. Like their container counterparts, tulips (hybrids only) are also lifted after spring flowering, but they are not replanted elsewhere in the garden. Instead, tulips are given a temporary trench before being dried off and stored for future planting. Other bulbs in need of storage include acidanthera, canna and ixia.

Frost is a danger to tuberous begonias and they must be brought in before the first one. Gladioli are also subject to frost damage, but only in severe cases. Otherwise they can be left to fend for themselves.

Storing bulbs is quite a simple operation, though there are different guidelines for varieties. Tulips are dried off for a few days. Any remaining earth, foliage, dying skin or small bulbs are removed. (Surface debris can cause rot to set in.) The bulbs are then put in an open box for good air circulation before being stored in a dry, cool place until autumn.

Before storing gladioli, cut the stems off while at the same time removing the old corms from the new ones. Store the corms in a frost-free environment, but make sure it is not too warm. With begonias, it is a case of storing the tubers in a box of peat (slightly moist) once their leaves have died.

Bulbs requiring storage are the exception. Most other types, left to their own devices, will produce ready-to-order flowers without too much gardening. Gardeners can help plants like crocuses and daffodils to prepare for subsequent spring flowering. Allow foliage to die down of its own accord, as the plants want to build up natural reserves from leaf material. A feed of fertiliser (liquid or granular) after flowering acts as a booster and further assists the plant's recovery rate. By ridding the plant of dead flowers and some of the stem, diversion of energy into seed formation is avoided. However, if self-seeding of crocuses and snowdrops is intended, leave the heads intact.

Bulbs do not favour very dry conditions. This applies both to spring and summer flowering types. Provide water if the ground appears not to offer enough moisture.

When lifting any bulbs for whatever reason, it is worth checking for fungi. Major forms are dry rot on gladioli and crocus, tulip fire on tulips, smoulder and narcissus fly on narcissi, and basal rot on other bulbs, including lilies. Burn any bulbs with disease as they can rot the entire crop.

A major feature of bulbs is their versatility. They can be taken up and replaced with another plant at a moment's notice. Fork out the bulbs and put them in another trench, covering about half their stems with soil. Replace the soil and allow foliage to die down. When ready for storage, lift in the normal fashion and keep them dry until autumn.

✵ ✵ ✵ ✵
Separating and Naturalising

Bulbs left to grow over a period of years accumulate smaller clusters of themselves. Separate the new bulbs and replant the originals after summer flowering. This serves two purposes. First, it maintains a spacious bed; and secondly it increases bulb stocks. As if to emphasise their value, the biggest of the new bulbs will produce a fresh bed of flowers after a few years. Most new bulbs should be replanted directly after division, but crocus and daffodil varieties can be sorted until regular planting time. Tulips and gladioli, though not subject to clumping, still produce offsets for propagation.

Naturalising bulbs is perhaps the most creative means of using them. Waste ground under trees provides the perfect setting for narcissi and crocus. The impact of seeing these flowers year after year enhances a part of the garden that might otherwise go fallow. Snowdrops have a similar part to play beside hedges.

Some of the more popular bulbs and corms are mentioned below.

A Selection of Bulbs, Corms and Tubers

◆   *Allium moly*
(Golden garlic)   An early summer plant with yellow flower sprays of 10in(25cm). Allow 4in(10cm) of space when planting during autumn.

◆   *Anemone coronaria*
(Windflower)   Has two types - single ('de Caen') and double ('St Brigid') strains. Bright flowers grows to 9in(23cm). Plant in autumn or spring and give 5in(13cm) space. Colour varies according to planting time.

◆   *Colchicum autumnale*
(Autumn crocus)   Flowers in autumn, with a crocus-type flower, pink in colour and 6-9in(15-23cm) high. Plant during summer with at least 9in(23cm) space.

◆   *Crinum x powellii*
White or pink lily-shaped flower which appears in late summer if planted in late spring. Usually 30in(75cm) high and needs 18in(45cm) space. Allow shelter.

◆   *Crocus*
All sorts to choose from. Plant in late summer, but be prepared for spring and autumn flowers. Needs sun and will produce a range of colours - white, yellow, blue. Height 5in(13cm). Space same.

◆   *Cyclamen coum*
Flowers of pink or white in winter. Should go down during early autumn, preferably with shade. Flowers 3in(8cm) tall. Space 5in(13cm).

◆ *Eranthis hyemalis*
(Winter aconite)   Another winter flower, this time with yellow dominant. Best planted in late summer in position of sun and shade. Grows 4in(10cm) with 3in(8cm) space.

◆ *Fritillaria meleagris*
(Snake's head fritillary)   Plant in autumn for a spring bell-shaped flower of chequered colours. Needs sun and shade to grow to its full 12in(30cm). Allow 6in(15cm) space.

◆ *Gladiolus*
(Sword lily)   Grows in many hybrid varieties. Summer miniatures enhance a rock garden. Take up and store corms in autumn. Spring planting is best, and the plants will grow from 18in(45cm) to 4ft(+1m). Give space of 4-6in(10-15cm).

◆ *Leucojum aestivum*
(Summer snowflake)   This is a white flower with greenish tips. If planted in late summer it will flower in spring at a height of 2ft(60cm). Allow 6in(15cm) space. Give sun and shade.

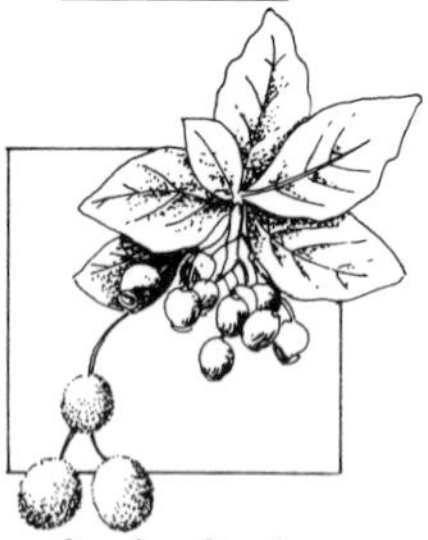

12. HERBACEOUS PERENNIALS

Few garden features tell more about the gardener than a herbaceous border. Choice reflects creativity and innovation, while presentation shows the extent of care and attention afforded to the garden. Creativity is indeed a noble virtue, but herbaceous perennials are also about application and patience. The displays of flowers in high summer are due reward for efforts made throughout the year.

Initial Care

Initially, perennials require little of the gardener's green fingers. They don't require largescale care and propagation. Rather like schoolchildren given the rules at the start, they behave impeccably. Sensible planting, tall behind short, means a colourful assembly. Moreover, providing a good choice of species is made to begin with, perennials continue to look their best in flower throughout summer.

Good students find it difficult to perform in cramped classrooms. Thus it is with perennials, which will want an open border with sufficient light and air. Strong growth is assured in a bed 4 ft(+1m) wide with plenty of sun.

Soil preparation is also important in guaranteeing a good display. Weeds are an unruly annoyance and must be cleared completely, using Weedol. Soil in herbaceous beds needs to settle before the incoming plants take root. Help the process along by adding Brown Gold and some lime if the soil is acidic.

Arranging the bed requires some thought in advance. Start by planning colour co-ordination, allowing for variety. Prior to planting, mark out perennial positions using small sticks. Dig a hole for each plant, using a spade or trowel according to root size. Plants look better when grouped in threes and fives, but make sure to allow space between each unit.

✹ ✹ ✹ ✹
Choosing the Plants

Choosing perennials is a matter of more than personal preference. While most garden centres have a fair selection of plants, some specialist outlets offer greater choice in hardy types. Even if the full range of perennials is available, better to choose shorter plants which suit normal-sized gardens. Shorter plants also require less staking than their taller counterparts. Perennials grown in plastic pots are fit for planting (weather and soil permitting) at any time during the year. Less cultivated varieties depend on special soil conditions in late autumn (light) and early spring (heavy) before they can go into the ground.

Growing perennials from seed is probably a more personal way to create a herbaceous border. There are other advantages in raising from seed, most notably expense. Seeds will survive if sown in a cold frame or outdoor bed, so there are no exceptional conditions required. Late spring and early summer are the best sowing times, but it will take a year before they flower. Some time after sowing, check for overcrowding and prick out seedlings if required. These can be replanted in the autumn.

✹ ✹ ✹ ✹
Care for Established Plants

Nurturing herbaceous varieties is a case of continuous assessment rather than end-of-term examination. Taller plants require a prop. A couple of bamboo canes tied to the stems with string prove an adequate support, but be sure to do this when the plant is half grown.

All sorts of things can cause the stems to bend, including water, so care is needed when providing moisture. Watering a perennial means keeping the soil moist at all times. Mulching is a sure way of keeping this condition in late spring and should help to guard against dry ground in summer.

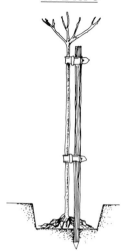

Taller perennials will require staking.

Healthy perennials do best with a balanced fertiliser diet applied in early spring. Use a 2oz(55g) per square yard(square metre) measurement and spread evenly across the bed. Hungry new plants may want more fertiliser.

Training and cutting is an important part of plant upkeep. In terms of support, thinning out weak shoots acts as an incentive to stronger growth among dominant ones. Dead heading, the practice of guillotining stems of failing flowers, maintains the plant's health by preventing it from setting seeds. It also spurs a second bloom among certain herbaceous varieties like lupins and pyrethrums. Cut back any other dead stems in autumn. Take the opportunity to root out persistent weeds. After cutting back, always boost the bed with compost and bonemeal. The latter should be applied in the same quantity as fertiliser.

There are always weak members of the herbaceous border - agapanthus, phygelius and schizostylis to name but three. These are especially sensitive to a drop in temperature, so keep them snug with a light blanket of straw. Chicken wire will secure the straw against wild winds.

Providing herbaceous perennials are guided and nurtured, there is no reason why the whole border should not bloom with flying colours come summer. Below are some varieties from which to choose. By medium height is meant 18in(45cm) to 3ft(1m). Average space is about 12in(30cm). Most plants are summer flowering and need sun.

Creative Herbaceous Perennials

◆ *Acanthus*
(Bear's breeches) Grows to 4ft(+1m) in height with flowers of white or purple spikes.

◆ *Aconitum*
(Monkshood) A tall perennial with blue or white spires in mid summer.

◆ *Agapanthus*
(African lily) Grows to 3ft(1m) at 30in(75cm) spacings with blue lily-type flowers. Wants sun.

◆ *Anemone*
(Windflower) Tall saucer-shaped flower with pink or white colours.

◆ *Aquilegia*
(Columbine) Very pointed flower of medium height and many colours.

◆ *Aster*
(Michaelmas daisy) Tall, needing plenty of space. Produces a range of colours: white, pink, red or blue. Some flower in autumn. Requires sun.

◆ *Astilbe*
3ft(1m) in height. Wants 2ft(60cm) of space. White or red plumes.

◆ *Campanula persicifolia*
(Bellflower) Wide range in height 2-5ft(60cm-1.5m) with white or blue bells. Looks for sun.

◆ *Chrysanthemum maximum*
(Shasta daisy) 3ft(1m) in height, 18in(45cm) space. White flower.

◆ *Convallaria*
(Lily of the valley)   Short plant producing white or pink bells in spring.

◆ *Coreopsis*
Short plant (18in/45cm) requiring similar area. Yellow daisy-like flowers need sun to bloom.

◆ *Delphinium*
One of the tallest plants (6ft/2m). A range of colourful flowers. Give sun and plenty of space.

◆ *Dianthus*
(Border carnations and pinks)   Very short height (9-12in/23-30cm). Allow 12-18in(30-45cm) space. Range from white to crimson flowers.

◆ *Dicentra*
(Bleeding heart)   As the name suggests, flowers are hanging reds and whites. Grows to medium height and flowers in late spring.

◆ *Echinopsis*
(Globe thistle)   3ft(1m) in height. Spiky heads, blue in colour.

◆ *Erigeron*
(Fleabane)   Medium height, multi-coloured, daisy-type flowers.

◆ *Euphorbia wulfenii*
(Spurge)   3-4ft(+1m). Yellow flower in late spring.

◆ *Geranium*
(Crane's bill)   Short, saucer-shaped flower of several colours. Likes sun and shade.

▲ *Herbaceous foliage in high summer.*

▲ *An eye-catching display of lupins.*

▲ *The muted beauty of stately delphiniums.*

▲ *Perfect harmony in a large rock garden.*

▲ *A delicate display of foxgloves*
(Digitalis).

▲ *A classical container sets off garden*
blooms.

▲ *Try grouping containers for a pleasing effect.*

▲ *Chrysanthemums and pansies do well in pots.*

▲ *The Japanese influence is seen in this water garden.*

▲ *A water garden designed by Classic Gardens.*

▲ *Marginal plants are happy in shallow water.*

▲ *Water lilies - favourites for any water garden.*

▲ *Soft brickwork and shades of green create a tranquil mood.*

▲ *A marvellous display of rhododendrons.*

▲ *Hanging baskets will enhance any setting.*

▲ *Dermot O'Neill with a selection of houseplants.*

◆ *Gypsophila paniculata*
(Baby's breath)   No baby at 4ft(+1m) high, needing a similar space. Masses of minute white or pink flowers. Wants sun.

◆ *Helleborus*
(Christmas rose)   Medium height, medium space which flowers in winter and spring. White or purple flowers come out in light shade.

◆ *Hemerocallis*
(Day lily)   Another plant of medium height with average space. Lily-like flowers produce a great range of colours which like sun and shade.

◆ *Hosta*
(Plantain lily)   Grows 1-3ft(up to 1m) high. Needs similar space. Likes light shade and sun.

◆ *Kniphofia*
(Red-hot poker)   Exactly as the name suggests, except for slightly varied yellow spikes. Grows 2-4ft(up to 1m). Wants 18in(45cm) between plants.

◆ *Lupinus*
(Lupin)   Tall plant up to 5ft(1.5m). Wants space of 2ft(60cm). Spires of many colours.

◆ *Mecanopsis*
3ft(1m) in height. Quite compact. Space of 9-18in(23-45cm). Turns out yellow or blue poppies in early summer.

◆ *Nepeta*
(Catmint)   Medium height, average spaced plant with a summer bloom of blue spikes.

◆ *Paeonia*
(Peony) Grows to 30in(75cm) in height, needs 2ft(60cm) space. A range of colours, including crimson and yellow.

◆ *Papaver orientale*
(Poppy) An early summer flower of 3ft(1m). Give good space and it will produce red, white or pink flowers in bowl-type shapes.

◆ *Penstemon*
Spiky flower in red varieties growing to 3ft(1m). With 18in(45cm) space between plants.

◆ *Phlox*
With sun and shade, this plant gives colourful clusters ranging from 2-4ft(up to 1m) high. Allow 18in(45cm) space.

◆ *Pyrethrum*
(Feverfew) No frenzy of colours, just white, pink or crimson flowers in early summer. Height 2ft(60cm), space 18in(45cm).

◆ *Salvia x superba*
Summer spikes of purple, 3ft(1m) in height. Give 2ft(60cm) space and sun for best flowers.

◆ *Stachys*
A short and compact plant. 12-15in(30-40cm). Useful silver leaves combine with purple flowers.

◆ *Veronica*
(Speedwell) 2ft(60cm) high with about 18in(45cm) space required for this perennial. It offers blue spires in summer.

❦❦❦❦
13. ROCK GARDENS

❦❦❦❦
A Natural Appearance

Of all the innovative approaches to landscaping, rock gardens portray a skill and sensitivity which is hard to compare. I believe a gardener must know the garden intimately in order to accommodate an Alpine feature which looks natural. Plants normally clinging for survival on mountain ledges might not look their best when laid out in a regular fashion in a tiny square of level garden. On the other hand, if tastefully arranged, such plants can enhance any location. In short, I would recommend some paperwork before the digging starts.

It is difficult, not to say impossible, to recreate a miniature Matterhorn at the back of the house. Likewise, a cost-cutting exercise such as a JCB-load of topsoil and a few dozen rocks thrown in for good measure create an ugly spectacle. In any case, rock plants demand growing conditions beyond this haphazard arrangement. Aim instead for an elevated bed wide enough to incorporate several plants. Start by laying a solid foundation covered with original top soil. Then, gradually build up a tiered rock formation using three-sided stones. Leave fissures or gaps between the rocks for plants. Continue building until you reach a point where the rock garden should go not further - before it becomes obtrusive.

❦❦❦❦
Positioning and Soil

Positioning is fundamental when considering a rock garden. Alpine features are the pride of any creative gardener, so make sure they can be enjoyed from indoors also. Sunlight on the true Alpine slopes is unlimited, so it should not be rationed to rock plants in the garden. Choose a well-drained slope (if there is one) facing southwest. This guarantees the best of the weather and the minimum of damp. It may be necessary to work on the drainage, but this is worth the effort as rock plants hate wet soil.

Depending on ground conditions in the garden, advice may be required with regard to suitable soil. Once more, think of the little plants way up there among the ski lodges and cowbells. Clay and heavy soil might be fine for potatoes, but rock plants look for something more refined, a rich mixture of sand, loam and peat. Grade the peat and sand according to moisture requirements.

Useful Alternatives

Of course not everyone can afford to develop a full rock garden. For instance, space might limit the extent to which a gardener can proceed. However, rock plants are worthy of inclusion anywhere. Because of their nature, some plants will value gaps along the patio (e.g. Arabis, Lychnis, Sedum), and in old or unused drinking troughs (most Alpines). Alternatively, wall fissures sometimes provide a good location if there is adequate drainage and it is joined with soil rather than mortar. Quite a number of plants find such walls an ideal habitat: Alyssum, Helianthemem, Iberis, Origanum and Sempervivum, to name but a few.

One of the more practical and creative presentations for rock plants is a raised bed. A foundation of small stones bordered by large rocks (to a height of three, lying horizontally) provides the basis for such a bed. Use the aforementioned Alpine soil both for plants and to cram the cracks between rocks. At this point, begin planting.

As might be expected from flowers well used to a fringe existence, rock plants are extremely adaptable. They will go into the ground at any time, except during freezing periods. Planting is relatively straightforward, but the plants may require a small amount of moisture if put in an arid spot.

✲✲✲✲
Caring for Rock Plants

Since there are few people around to look after them atop a 6000ft mountain, rock plants do not expect luxury treatment. But they will appreciate a little care. Save them from mud bombardment by putting several centimetres of tiny pebbles (any type except limestone) over bare soil. Give the plants a ration of food once a year from whatever stock of plant nutrient available. In times of drought, water sufficiently. Guard against slugs and weeds which can lay waste any collection of Alpines. There are a number of plants averse to winter's damp which may need plastic covering. In this latter group, Androsace and Lewisia are perhaps the most notable.

The Pasque flower — one of the first Alpines to appear.

When the snow starts to melt and St Bernards take a well-earned break, Alpine plants come out in force. Though the location may differ, late spring and summer are still popular flowering times for a whole range of plants in the rock garden. One of the first to appear is *Pulsatilla vulgaris* (Pasque flower) in large blooms of purple and gold. *Aethionema* 'Warley Rose' with its pink flowers is next to show, while *Lewisia cotyledon's* white, pink, yellow or red blooms are not far behind. Summer sees a multitude of rock plants in flower. *Lithospermum diffusum* produces a spectacular blue shade, while *Sempervivum* (Houseleek) provides the perfect complement with a sophisticated pink flower.

There are many other rock plants to choose from, all offering colour and interest to transform a modest garden.

14. MELLOW FRUITFULNESS

In a creative sense, fruit offers some of the most tangible evidence of worthwhile effort. Although my own garden does not lend itself to fruit growing, I have always admired the dedication others have shown in pursuit of excellence. Whether it is in selection or planting, cultivation or harvesting, fruit trees demand care and attention.

Not so long ago, while advising a friend on the development of a small orchard, it occurred to me how few people realise apple trees do not grow on their own roots. Instead, it is the nurseryman who prepares the ground, so to speak. He develops 'stocks' or special root systems by grafting. Dwarf stocks are by far the most popular as they produce compact trees with an early crop.

Planting Fruit Trees

Planting fruit trees is straightforward, provided general rules are followed. Plant bare-rooted fruit trees in late October. To begin, dig a hole three feet(1m) across, spreading the roots and planting firmly. Take care not to bury the union between stock and shoot of the tree used to form a graft. Otherwise, all value of a special stock will be lost as the variety sends out its own roots. Try to plant trees nine feet(3m) apart in an average-sized garden, or twelve feet(3.5m) for a larger one. Bear in mind that the excess ground between tree rows needs attention.

Tending new apple trees involves some important steps. In February, prune most of the leaders to about half way, just above a bud. In early April or May, put a two-inch(5cm) mulch of moss peat or well-rotted compost around each tree. It may be necessary to stake the tree, particularly one of the special stocks. Shallow and fibrous roots on several stocks sometimes cause the tree to blow over. This might happen in exposed gardens subject to high winds, or when the crop is weighted to one side.

❊ ❊ ❊ ❊
Fruit Varieties

Apples have aristocratic names to describe the varieties. Early Worcester, Fortune, Laxton's Superb and Ellison's Orange are all high-class dessert apples. Also in this category, and deservedly so, Cox's Orange Pippins reputedly contribute to a superb apple pie.

Most kinds of pear require a pollinator, but a few are self fertile. Among the latter class, take note of Conference, William Bon Chrétien and Fertility. Laxton's Superb produces a heavy crop of sweet and juicy pears for early September.

Among self-fertile plums, Victoria is a popular dessert variety in small gardens. Dennison's Superb is highly-rated, while the regally-named Czar makes a good cooker.

❊ ❊ ❊ ❊
When to Pick

Picking fruit requires almost as much attention as growing. For example, quality dessert pears must be harvested before they ripen on the trees. Otherwise the flavour will be impaired. Knowing when to harvest pears is important. With early to mid-season fruit, pick before the green base turns yellow. Alternatively, lift a pear to see if the stalk breaks gently from the spur.

Disease is a major concern, especially with plum trees. By pruning in summer, plums are guarded against silver leaf disease entering through wounds. Healthy plums also appreciate two applications of fertiliser, one in June and the other in September.

Fruit growers seem to derive immense satisfaction from their efforts. Perhaps this is because growing apples, pears and plums tests a gardener's knowledge to the full. I mention particularly John Conan, formerly of Marlfield Garden Centre, who likes nothing better than to pick fruits from his own trees. John is a fine gardener who imparted some of his wealth of knowledge to me, especially on the subject of fruit.

The following chart is a checklist of fruit tree varieties, their season of use and remarks.

Apples, Dessert

Name	Season of Use	Remarks
American Mother	Oct. - mid Jan.	High quality
Charles Ross	Sept. - Nov.	Large fruit, good flavour
Cox's Orange Pippin	Oct. - Dec.	Excellent flavour
Ellison's Orange	Sept. - Oct.	Very juicy
James Grieve	Sept.	Pollinating variety
Laxton's Superb	Jan. - March	Good flavour
Worcester Pearmain	Sept.	Pollinating variety

Pears

Name	Season of Use	Harvesting Time
Conference	Oct. - Nov.	End Sept.
Doyenné du Comice	Oct. - Nov.	Early Oct.
Durondeau	Oct. - Nov.	End Sept.
William Bon Chrétien	Sept.	End Sept.
Fertility	Sept. - Oct.	Early Sept.
Laxton's Superb	August	Mid August

Plums

Name	Season of Use	Remarks
Czar	Early August	Culinary
Victoria	Late August - Early September	Good pollinator
Rivers Early	Early August	Culinary
Early Laxton	July	Dessert or culinary

* * * *

15. CONTAINER PLANTS

While the garden is a major focus of attention for any creative gardener, perhaps the finer touches can be seen elsewhere. I refer particularly to plant arrangements in hanging baskets, pots, window boxes and so forth. No more than a golfer playing a chip shot par excellence or a tennis player hitting a drop volley with finesse, so the elegant container of plants speaks volumes about a gardener's instinct.

* * * *
Choosing Containers

Making use of landscape seems to be the most effective way of deploying containers. Take the bare look off gable walls by hanging baskets of ivy-leaf geraniums, pansies and lobelia. Unused rain barrels, so often neglected, can be turned to good use when home to spring plants like wallflowers and forget-me-nots. Window boxes full of crocuses and irises look especially pretty when placed on a downstairs ledge, particularly if the window is large.

Unusual containers, discretely placed, sometimes say more about a gardener's style than five flower beds. Perhaps a stepladder, once in demand but now lying idle, could get a new lease of life as a trellis for climbing plants like clematis varieties.

Some ideas are unusual, some ready-made. What they all have in common are possibilities for the gardener to show skill and flair. Besides offering chances for creative displays, pots and tubs of plants also bring garden fragrances closer to the house. Blooms of colour around the house impress like a new coat of paint on the front door or whitewash on the wall. Plants get a new role beyond pretty beds and borders.

There are a number of points regarding containers about which gardeners should be aware. Most obvious is securing heavy pots and baskets to walls and ledges. In the case of window boxes and hanging baskets, it is a good idea to attach them with a hook and eye. Timber boxes sometimes require internal and external protection to prevent rot (this type of box should never touch the ground for the same reason). Owing to their relatively artificial situation, container plants will probably need more than the regular garden soil. Choose a peaty compost - Shamrock Multipurpose or Shamrock Tree and Shrub.

✲ ✲ ✲ ✲
Creative Use

Creative use of containers can turn the ordinary garden into something special, yet plants need attention and maintenance to look their best. For example, hanging baskets in sunny spots need daily watering during summer. The condition of flowers is an obvious indicator that water is required, though the weight of the basket is more immediate in telling when to add moisture. When watering, compost should dry out to stop waterlogging.

A good drainage system should be built into larger containers. Layer the bottom with pieces of brick and keep the container off the ground to allow proper drainage. Wooden beams or large rocks act as good supports for big containers such as barrels.

Compost is the lifeblood of container plants, a point worth remembering. Do not spare compost; rather fill up containers leaving some space right at the top. Some shrubs will need a compost floor to establish their roots. Firm this compost around the roots before adding more. Bear in mind that perennials get a spring compost change. Most container plants appreciate a liquid feed every couple of weeks. Use Miracle-Gro, mixing one heaped tablespoon to one gallon of water. For lime-hating plants, try Miracid at the same rate. This will keep your plants in top condition.

16. WATER GARDENS

Eastern influences on gardening are far and wide, and the Japanese are credited with promotion of water gardens. Perhaps it is a combination of Oriental rainfall patterns and a sensitive feel for nature that has led the people of Japan to emphasise water features. Wherever the explanation lies, few can deny the impressive contribution which pools and ponds make to the surroundings. In terms of creativity, there are few outward expressions to compare with a water garden.

Many people are put off garden pools by thoughts of long hours digging holes, leakage, tedious cleaning - and ultimately a white elephant. True, water gardens are serious business; they need attention and therefore take up time. However if properly planned and developed, most concerns give way to an outstanding garden addition. Indeed the only real argument against a pool is if young children play in the vicinity. Otherwise there is no reason not to consider water as a viable proposition providing space is available.

✿✿✿✿
Preparing the Pool

Begin by digging the pool. 10ft x 8ft(2.5 x 3m) is the optimum size, down to about 18in(45cm) in depth. With such measurements, pool maintenance presents fewer problems. Shape is not an issue, but try to avoid the extreme ornamental types on offer in garden centres. Allow a steep underwater drop to a ledge 8in(20cm) below the water level. A ledge width of 9in(23cm) provides the perfect stand for plants which grow in shallow water.

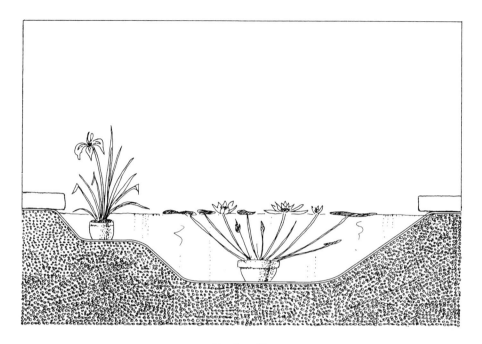

Pond profile.

Options for pool insulation vary from the popular butyl rubber to the older concrete method. All liners have some problem or other. Concrete, though very neat looking, takes up a lot of time and effort. Even then, there is the possibility of minute fractures caused by frost and dirt. Extra-strong polythene gives good service, but must be replaced almost annually. Although easy to position, size is the major trouble with the made-to-measure pools. Usually constructed with fibre glass, these pools are frequently too small to be anything more than a minor feature in gardening terms. Butyl rubber sheeting therefore offers the soundest alternative. Easy to put down (though make sure the surface is smooth and free from stones which might puncture it), butyl will need attention at the edges where a rim above the waterline remains visible.

Many of the problems regarding water supply have disappeared with the advent of pumps. The original water is pumped continuously around, so keeping a regulated temperature and content for plants and fish. It should be said that pumps are not a fundamental requirement for maintaining a water garden. Pools always look their best when filled to the brim. For this reason it may be necessary to add fresh water with a hose. For more elaborate aspects like fountains or miniature waterfalls, there are special pumps to do the job.

It is very important to site the pool in a suitable spot. Sunken areas are out because the water pressure from the soil could upset pool liners. Parts of the garden close to trees can prove a problem because of elongated roots and falling leaves. The ideal spot is a sun trap, preferably near a rock garden.

❈ ❈ ❈ ❈
Choosing the Plants

There is no limit to the creative approach gardeners may employ with water. Different plants thrive on the ledges or deep in the recesses. A rock garden provides the perfect platform from which to start a tiered descent to the pool. Along the ledges just beneath the water level, try the colourful array of *Caltha palustris* (Marsh marigold), *Iris laevigata* and *Alisima plantago* (Water plantain). Deep water plants are those which grow at depths of 12-18in(30-45cm). Among this category are the ever-popular water lilies (a large range available) and the more select types like *Aponogeton distachyos* (Water hawthorn).

It is important to keep the pool clear of algae, especially with fish. Submerged plants such as *Potmogeton* can help with this task and give oxygen to fishlife as well. Floating plants complete the water garden effect, with *Azolla caroliniana* (Fern) and *Hydrocharis morsus ranae* (Frogbit) two good selections.

Pools prove the most interesting habitat for a wide range of life. Plants can be supplemented with various types of fish. The pool itself is likely to attract its own colourful clientele - frogs, rare birds and so forth.

Gardens take on a new life with the arrival of water. Besides the colour of water plants, there are the added reflections from existing flowers. The pool brings out the best of the weather. Cloud formations mirrored on the water surface and blue sky illuminated even further in the garden are other advantages for pool owners. Then there are the sounds, cascading splashes providing an additional tone to complement the singing blackbirds. All told, water gardens create a mood unrivalled by other features.

✽✽✽✽
Seasonal Care for Pools

As the seasons change, the pool, like the garden, responds. Plant life takes its cue from the water, fish sense a change in the weather, while oxygen content is determined by seasonal conditions. The gardener, whose job it is to ensure continuity, must be alive to developments from the first hint of spring to the last breath of winter.

One of the first indications that spring has arrived to the pool is the invasion of algae. However, this bark is worse than the bite. The green water looks nasty, but is in fact harmless to pool inhabitants and best left alone. Algae grow when the temperatures rise and there is plenty of oxygen available. Spring is the opportune time for algae since the other plants like lilies have not started to grow and are therefore not oxygenating.

New pools should get their first quota of marginal plants in late spring. With the season progressing and milder weather coming in, fish abandon their slumbers. Feed them now, because it guards against fungal infection later in the year. The pool will appreciate a spring clean every few years. When cleaning, give the fish a temporary but secure pool made from polythene. Take the opportunity to divide water lilies. To do this, sever small growing shoots from the original crown and plant in good soil.

Marginal plants and water lilies come into their own in summer. Plant while there is plenty of daylight and warm, still water. Unfortunately, blanket weed likes these conditions too, so clear it out before it gets hold of the plants. Any plant casualties which do result should be removed before they pollute the water and cause even more damage. In very hot conditions, fish may be gasping for oxygen. Fresh splashing water sprayed from a hose or a waterfall helps increase the oxygen content and keeps the fish satisfied.

With autumn approaching, fish need protection. Their main concern is aerial bombardment from falling leaves and dead material from water plants. Oxygen content decreases, and toxic gases are released from rotting vegetation. By placing wire mesh above the pool surface, tree and plant leaves are trapped before they reach the water. The gardener would also do well to clear any fallen leaves and cut off dead lily stems. A special fish nutrient (available from pet shops or garden centres) administered regularly in small quantities keeps the fish in good health. Elsewhere, waterside plants should come down, and submersible pumps should come up. Disconnect surface pumps and store carefully.

Winter is a time of sleep and relaxation for plants and fish. The same is not true for the gardener. Though fish do not require food, or plants around the pool tending, vigilance is called for against ice formation. Fish can withstand cold temperatures but may perish if the pool freezes over. Toxic gases of decomposing material are trapped by the ice mass and suffocate the fish. Smashing the ice with a spade will only serve to shock fish to death, so a pool heater is the best answer. Pool heaters are easy to operate and keep an ice-free area in times of extreme cold. Ice can also cause damage to concrete pool beds and walls as a result of water expansion. Several small balls floating on the surface can absorb pressure increases in freezing temperatures.

17. LAWN CARE

To cut or not to cut - that is the question. Well...one of the questions. I meet a good number of people who believe lawn upkeep goes no further than a cut once a fortnight. Nothing could be further from the truth. Though the lawn does not stand out as an entity in the creative sphere, it still affects all the beds, borders and rock gardens around it. As such, it is an integral part of creative gardening and deserves equal attention. In other words, mowing a lawn is not the final word.

Lawn Care

Lawn conditions are very much dictated by the soil underneath. Grass may cry out for nutrients and moisture on a regular basis, especially if its soil is grainy. On the other hand, the earth may be packed in heavy clumps. In this case, fork marks in the lawn relieve the groaning mass below and allow the ground to breathe or drain.

When hot sun beats the ground, and before grass protests too much by fading or scorching, water the soil. The chief worry is that parched topsoil might turn off the life support system, leaving grass irreparably damaged. A water sprinkler is the best method of getting moisture down to the roots in even quantities. However a hose with an adaptable head will do quite well.

Though water helps to keep grass looking green, it is also a good idea to feed a lawn with fertiliser once a year. The transition between spring and summer is the best time to consider this task. Choose a fertiliser with long-lasting effects. Garden centres have a wide range and in most cases, someone there will advise on the best treatment. Usually the preference is for a compound fertiliser containing potash and phosphate. This mixture provides lawns with important nutrients over a long period. In order to get maximum benefit from the fertiliser, avoid applying on wet days, but make sure the soil is relatively soft. Methods of application vary, depending on whether the fertiliser is granular or liquid.

✿✿✿✿
Seasonal Requirements

Autumn is a busy time for working on the lawn. One way to tidy the appearance of the grass is to rake away the season's 'thatch' or debris resulting from mowing. A long-pronged rake is most suitable for this job, since it helps to pick up bits of old grass which often go unnoticed with regular raking. Thorough raking like this, followed up again in the spring, helps maintain a good lawn appearance. Similarly the application of a top dressing benefits grass condition. A light coating of compost, peat and sand distributed evenly over the grass keeps a level surface.

Spring sees the start of the cutting season but this should not occasion toil and trouble. If a number of simple rules are remembered, good grass growth and verdant splendour are assured. Begin with a once-weekly cut in spring, double this in summer, and revert back to one mowing during autumn. It is important to adjust the height of mower blades to 1in(2.5cm) at the height of summer and about 3/4in(2cm) for autumn. Regulating the blades helps retain an adequate grass cover in arid conditions while reducing the chances of weed growth at other times. Damp grass is a handicap to a good cut, while leftover mowings also prove a hindrance.

Though the gardener may not be ready to give away his or her kingdom for a lawnmower, there are few items which rate more useful. A trusty mower can cut work by half. Cylinder mowers may look old-fashioned, but they give an extremely neat finish. Many people are attracted to them because of a striped-lawn effect left as the mower's rollers travel across the grass. However, it should be noted that the cylinder has poor blade power with a tendency to blunt. Rotary or motor mowers are quite popular, especially in rental establishments. Before going to work with a rotary, check its two blades for consistency. Owing to operations in long grass (where this mower is most valuable), rotary blades often come into contact with stones or rocks. This sometimes results in damaged blades and, subsequently, tufts or an uneven cut. Hover mowers move via a cushion of air. A streamlined mower, the hover manages to get into tight corners and awkward places. This machine is more suited to short grass.

✿✿✿✿
A Lawn Checklist

To ensure a well-kept lawn, it is worth keeping a duty checklist for each season. Winter work starts with a general clean-up of leaves and twigs. Use a long-pronged rake for this job. Lay turf if soil is dry. Restrict lawn activities as the season ends. Instead, it might be a good idea to give the lawnmower a preliminary service. Towards the end of winter, prepare soil for any new grass, but wait to grow seed until spring. At this stage, give the motor mower a good mechanical overhaul in readiness for the cutting season.

Spring rings in changes and the lawn is no exception. Grass growth is on the increase, so trim the lawn with a light cut. More frequent and sharp cutting can take place as the season advances. Sow seed once the sun starts to heat the ground sufficiently. Early spring sowing is acceptable, but mid season is better. Improved weather conditions also mean moss may make an appearance, so put down a prepared treatment if required. Weeds are on a spring offensive and weedkiller should be used to combat any problem areas. Likewise, apply fertiliser towards season's end.

Summer sees a lot of growth and although weekly cuttings are the general rule, there are exceptions. Heatwaves, for example, mean extra lawn-care. In this case more watering, fertilisers and cautious mowing are the order of the day. Weeds could still be a problem, so continue treatment. As summer draws to a close, preparations for a new lawn are set in motion. After digging, wait until the first crop of weeds are up and out before applying fertiliser. Then, sow grass seed.

Early autumn is a time of rapid growth in new lawns. This will continue until the weather turns cold. Carry out any running repairs on bald patches, while clearing dead material with a vigorous raking. Air topsoil and feed the lawn through the season. The final act in lawn care comes with a thorough cleaning of the mower before it is stored in a safe, dry place.

18. BONSAI – MINIATURE TREES FROM THE ORIENT

Bonsai, the art of growing trees in miniature, certainly deserves a place in a book on creative gardening. The word comes from two Japanese words, *bon* and *sai,* meaning a shallow pan and plant - or, by implication, an artificially dwarfed tree.

The ancient Japanese practice started when tiny tree specimens were dug out of cliffs and mountain slopes. Such was the remarkable resemblance to the regular forest trees, early gardeners were encouraged to perfect the art of growing the little trees in simulated conditions.

The evolution of bonsai over the centuries culminated in its huge popularity throughout the world. An appealing aspect of bonsai is the way it can be practised without a garden. This would account for its attraction in crowded countries like Japan, but this is not in itself the sole explanation. In truth, bonsai is an absorbing hobby and a very good investment (value increases annually) considering the negligible cost. However, it is worth remembering that only genuine bonsai are of any value and should be perfect examples of tree forms.

✿ ✿ ✿ ✿
Propagation

While bonsai are available from specialist outlets in Ireland, much enjoyment can be had in growing your own. Gardeners will need an abundance of patience and a good eye for line to get involved with bonsai.

The option of whether to grow from seed (this method is known as *Misho*) or cuttings (*Sashiki*) presents the first major decision. Cuttings give faster results, but seeds can produce a more interesting range.

Some of the larger seed merchants in Dublin supply both mixed and named varieties of seeds especially suitable for bonsai growing. A good idea is to start with a wide variety of seeds as this allows for shedding the less interesting ones as they develop. Note deciduous and evergreens have different germination patterns. While deciduous take one or two months to germinate, evergreens take between two and three. For the first year of growth, regular watering is the only requirement.

In terms of growth, cuttings have several years' head start over seeds and give a clear impression of what the bonsai will eventually look like. There is no problem in selecting cuttings as they can be taken from any tree, but be careful to cut at the right time of the year, usually early spring or autumn. Cuttings should be about 3 inches(7.5cm) long. I find hormone rooting powder is beneficial in stimulating bonsai root growth. During the second year, the bonsai will take shape. It needs a lot of attention. First, it must be repotted and this usually takes place in late winter or early spring. Any new growth must be twisted and trained into shape by means of wires and cautious pruning. Once established, bonsai need this treatment every two or three years.

✿✿✿✿
Essential Care

Care is the essential ingredient for growing successful trees. Choosing the correct container is an important start. Make sure it is shallow, and square or rectangular in form with at least one drainage hole. Try to get a container which is not glazed. Size is another factor since it determines the amount of soil the roots have to occupy and so limits the growth of the plant.

Pruning roots becomes necessary only when the tap root is too large for the pot; otherwise feeding roots are best left alone.

Bonsai need water daily (twice a day in summer) because of their small ration of soil. Unless they receive a full quota of water, the plants will die. One way to ensure an adequate supply of water is to stand porous pots in a tray of water. Once the plant is established, it can be left out to gather moisture from the rain and dew. However, guard against excessive sun and frost.

The plants require a period of low temperatures while resting in winter since these are the conditions of their natural habitat. Bonsai growers always consider the habitat factor. In Japan, for example, trees are kept outdoors for most of the year. They are only brought in on rare occasions. Irish gardeners should consider copying their Japanese counterparts by growing several bonsai and rotating their indoor spells.

Training bonsai involves pruning shoots and wiring branches. In spring when the tips of new shoots appear to be about 1 inch(2.5cm) long, they are constantly removed or pinched out. The practice of pinching is repeated on secondary growth, noticeable by its small leaves. This takes place in early to mid-summer.

Wiring the tree helps to twist and wind it into the desired shapes. Strong copper wire is fastened to the trunk and branches and then attached to pegs in the compost or to other wires around the outside of the container. Deciduous trees are wired in summer, evergreens in winter.

✿ ✿ ✿ ✿

19. HOUSEPLANTS

For many people, pot plants are true companions. Like any other long term occupant of the house, however, plants must be in harmony with their surroundings and their comrades. In other words, they need a suitable place to live and proper care and attention from their owner. Plant buyers should think carefully about both these aspects rather than purchasing on impulse. Just because the plant looks marvellous in the garden centre is no guarantee in itself. A quality plant is one with plenty of buds still to come, lending itself to creative use. The following are some of the most popular house plants available.

◆ *Azaleas*

An exclusive plant with a price to match, the azalea is slow-growing and needs heat to force it into bloom. The *Azalea indica* rates among the favourites in this variety. A delicate sort, *Azalea indica* is fussy about temperatures. It should not be put out until the last chill of spring frost is gone. Indoors, the plant will do best in cool conditions. Azaleas are not hardy and will die in dry air or when they are thirsty. Central heating poses a problem, but a plant steeped in damp peat with fine water sprayed on its leaves will survive. However, azaleas are not partial to overwatering and will display a dislike by turning brown and spotted. As if to

turning brown and spotted. As if to emphasise their fastidious nature, the plant requires rain rather than tap water because of the lime content in the latter. Growth will continue with regular watering even after flowering.

Different seasons bring different demands. In spring, give azaleas shade in the garden. Summer is spent complete with clay pot plunged in ground water and is also a time of regular feeding. Nutriment is provided in autumn, but indoors at a temperature of 55-60°F(13-18°C).

♦ *Winter Cherry*
Discretion in choosing house plants is nowhere more important than with *Solanum* (Winter cherry) and its cousin, *Capsicum*. While it may look just the picture for a dull winter's day, bear in mind the poisonous berries, especially if there are children in the house.

Plenty of water, a 3-4in(8-10cm) pot, and cool temperatures keep *Solanum* happy. To maintain a good coat of berries and leaves, give the plant plenty of light.

♦ *Cyclamen*
The indoor gardener is spoiled for choice here, thanks to the miracles of modern science. From the older cyclamen which only flowered after fifteen months, modern varieties now bloom in nine, while F1 hybrids reach full growth in half a year. Original cyclamen grown from seed were a substantial plant in their 5-6in(12-15cm) pots, but the new types are less impressive with smaller containers. Hybrids have a typical uniform habit and early flowering is a positive advantage.

Though the choice of cyclamen may vary, routine upkeep should not. Watering is vital, since the foliage and corm must never get wet. Allow the plant to drink by standing the pot in a bowl of water. Remove from water once the top compost is moist. A container of damp peat provides another way of keeping cyclamens in fine fettle. For best results, immerse the plant pot into the peat and leave it there until good humidity transfer has taken place. Needless to say, these actions will also promote a cool temperature very favourable to cyclamens.

Maintain the plant's leaf structure by carefully removing any yellow leaves or faded flower. Take care to detach all such growth to prevent future rot. Feed winter-flowering cyclamens one day a week, with half-strength liquid nutrient added to water.

◆ *Poinsettia*

A big red flowering plant, poinsettia is associated largely with Christmas. Though most people think the plant is only a festive visitor, it is possible to keep one for another year. Proper care in the beginning and correct treatment after flowering help prolong growth.

Poinsettias are similar to cyclamen in that they like moisture. Again, plunge the plant into a pot of moss peat to ensure a supply of humidity. Feed is required every week until the colour bracts fade and the plant needs a rest.

To maintain poinsettia for a longer period, cut them back to within six inches of soil after flowering takes place. Guarantee warm surroundings for the plant, freedom from wet and draughty conditions. Leave it in this place for about six weeks without watering. After signs of growth appear, return to normal watering and feeding. As autumn arrives, but before coloured bracts show, give the plant no more than ten hours' light per day. It is a good idea, perhaps, to leave poinsettia in a dark, unused room during the night. While the plant likes warm temperatures (65-70°F/18-21°C), it is not over enamoured with life in the lounge.

Poinsettias are grown from cuttings taken in mid-summer and rooted in a closed, heated propagating frame. A good quality plant is expensive. Yet the attractive display outweighs the cost. Top market types will have three plants grown in a five inch pot. The effect created is an appealing bush of flowers.

The feeding of your houseplants during their growing season is most important, as this will promote healthy and strong growth especially with established plants. I use Miracle Gro plant feed at the rate of one teaspoon in four pints of water.

❀ ❀ ❀
20. YEAR PLANNER

A month-by-month plan to guide you through the gardening year

Each January, gardeners everywhere turn their thoughts to the work ahead. The cold and wet conditions (not to mention the shortage of daylight) don't encourage an all-out assault on gardening tasks. Instead, I find it more profitable to divide my time between essential duties and drawing up a checklist of jobs to be tackled in subsequent months. This allows scope for a creative gardening approach.

❀ ❀ ❀
January

Winter digging marks an undemanding return to the garden after a Christmas break. Make sure to firm in perennials and shrubs lifted by the frost. Phlox and Oriental poppies are ready for root cuttings. Pruning in January includes jasmine, outdoor vines and wisteria (after flowering). Sow cauliflower and onions in the heated greenhouse; sweet pea in pots covered by unheated glass.

❀ ❀ ❀
February

Fruit and vegetables dominate activities. Spray against pests/disease threatening apples and pears using Clean Up. Plant fruit trees. Cloche strawberries for early cropping. Bring stored dahlia tubers into growth for cuttings. Pruning in February is divided between roses and autumn raspberries. Sow tomatoes and French beans in a heated greenhouse; broad beans, peas, carrots and brussels sprouts in the garden. Outdoor vegetables should be well protected.

****
March

March is a month for planting and sowing. Outside, plant potatoes and gladioli corms. Grow tomatoes in the heated greenhouse using Shamrock Growbags. Continue to plant and prune fruit trees. Sow half-hardy annuals such as salvia, aster, ageratum and petunia in Multipurpose Compost. Vegetable sowing includes lettuce, parsnips, onions, leeks and spinach. It is timely to take cuttings from dahlia tubers started in February. Back in the greenhouse, harden off sweet peas. Last but not least, feed top and soft fruits with sulphate of ammonia.

****
April

The garden is beginning to take shape. With this in mind, attention turns to developing a new lawn. Also in the landscaping vein, April is the ideal month to plant evergreen conifers and shrubs. On the vegetable front, prepare a trench for celery while sowing sweetcorn, runnerbeans and marrows in the heated greenhouse. It should be remembered that the greenhouse is subject to high temperatures, so take care to ventilate. Continue to sow lettuce as demand might soon exceed supply. Sweet pea's sojourn indoors is over; plant out in April. Looking forward to summer, take flowers off spring strawberries.

****
May

A busy month ahead with a whole range of tasks. The best start is the replacement of old bedding plants with summer flowers. Outdoor flowering chrysanthemum should be grown in the garden during May. Lift polyanthus and propagate by division. Sunny conditions mean shading is required in the greenhouse. While working under glass, sow cinerarias and primula. Attend to berries. Start by tying in the growing shoots of blackberries and hybrid varieties. Gooseberries are prone to attack by pests, so protect by spraying (the same applies to peaches). Vegetables requiring treatment against pests are turnips, carrots and onions. In a quiet sowing month, cucumber, parsnip, broccoli and beetroot appear to be the main candidates.

❊ ❊ ❊ ❊
June

The height of summer should be a spectacular and colourful time in the garden. Add to effect with individual hanging baskets. Displays of Sweet William and wallflowers are best prepared when sown in the open. Elsewhere, *Begonia rex* and African violet are two flowers from which to take leaf cuttings. While the warm sun and dashing colour brighten days in the garden, the dry weather takes its toll on outdoor crops, so remember to water them. Fruit also requires attention; be ever vigilant for pests using Rose Clear. Ordinary gardening jobs are almost as plentiful as summer flowers. Continue sowing vegetables. Stake peas and beans. Plant tomatoes, onions, cucumber and brussels sprouts.

❊ ❊ ❊ ❊
July

The emphasis in July is very much on special duties. *Clematis montana* are liable to branch congestion, so prune to ease crowding. Check gladioli and dahlia are well staked. In the greenhouse, coleus is ready for cuttings. All sorts of organisms are on the march. Particularly vulnerable to attack are apples and celery, the former from codling moth, the latter from leaf spot. In both cases Rose Clear acts as a deterrent. There is no rest from sowing vegetables. At least there is some reward when harvesting begins with shallots. The little onions should also be dried. Meanwhile, raspberries, redcurrants, apples and pears all require a summer pruning.

❊ ❊ ❊ ❊
August

As the year unfolds, so gardening tasks become more diverse. This is the month to stock the compost heap with waste matter from the kitchen and soft plants. Working with cuttings, gardeners will propagate roses and take them semi-ripe from shrubs. Transplanting Sweet William and wallflower is next on the agenda. Plant out colchicum bulbs for autumn flowering. Continuing the flower theme, sow cyclamen and schizanthus seeds in the greenhouse using Shamrock Multipurpose Compost. August is the last opportunity to sow vegetables. It is also the month to plant savoys and strawberries. Finally, spray cherries and blackcurrants against pests.

❀❀❀❀
September

Caution is urged turning into autumn, not least in the greenhouse. Maintain constant temperatures through careful ventilation and remove any dead material or leaves. Check all other greenhouse plants. Looking towards a lawn, take the opportunity to sow grass seed. Focus attention on well-rooted pelargoniums - it is time to pot them up. September activities would not be complete without taking in stocks of fruit and vegetables. Harvest and store maincrop carrot, apples and pears. Earth up celery and leeks for blanching. With an eye to next year, put greasebands on apple and pear trees. When pruning blackberry, make sure to retain the new wood.

❀❀❀❀
October

The cold weather is setting in, a signal to work overtime before winter hits full force. Begin by lifting dahlias immediately after the first frost. Store dahlia tubers and gladioli corms. Take out bedding plants and put spring bulbs in. If landscaping plans include herbaceous perennials, then plant them out in light soil with a little Brown Gold. Roses and gooseberries share at least one thing in common - hardwood cuttings should be taken from both during October. Tomatoes are next on list. Pick now for indoor ripening. It is an appropriate time to propagate and replant rhubarb. Main crops to be lifted and stored are potatoes, turnips, beetroot and swedes.

❀❀❀❀
November

Though this is traditionally a sombre month, there is a sign of hope in gardening activities, most of which relate to preparation for next year. Winter digging is a case in point, so commence this month. Similarly if a hedge is intended, get the soil ready in advance. Deciduous leaves lie on the ground, casualties of winter's onslaught. Use them to make leaf mould. Start pruning established apple and pear trees. Finish pruning hybrid berries, blackberries, raspberries and blackcurrants. Over in the greenhouse, chrysanthemums have flowered, so cut them down. Roses will appreciate cut backs if only to prevent rocking in the wind.

Most cacti will not be crying out for water. The lone exception looking for a good drink is the Christmas cactus.

✤ ✤ ✤ ✤
December

All sorts of plans are made for Christmas, but a gardener should not neglect an order list for next year. Seed catalogues offer suggestions, so take time out to search through the range. Meanwhile, back in the garden, work remains. If there is no frost, plant roses in prepared soil using Brown Gold. On the other hand herbaceous perennials prefer light soil, so continue planting the variety. Dahlia tubers are subject to rot, so check the stock carefully. Fruit trees will want a manure mulch in December. Hungry nectarines or peaches appreciate an early Christmas lunch of nitrogen and potash. Before sprouts and carrots play their part in Yuletide festivities, why not plan where to sow next year's vegetable crop? Break up any ice in the garden pond as fish need air. Finally, enjoy the well-deserved Christmas break.

ACKNOWLEDGMENTS

I am indebted to more people than I can mention for their help and encouragement in writing this book.

I would like to thank Patrick Kelly for all the thought and caring work he put into it. I am also very grateful to my friend Paul Marsden for his kindness and patience in reading my type script. I would like to set down here my gratitude to photographer John Cooney for his splendid photographs and his enthusiasm and skill. For their encouragement and patience, I would like to say a very warm thank you to Noel Smith who has always given me the chance to express my creative ideas and to Agnes Cogan, Brendan Leason, Barbara Carolin and all the staff who work on 'Live at 3'.

I would like to thank Michael Gill and especially my editor, Roberta Reeners, who has not only shown remarkable tolerance but who has been an unfailing source of help and encouragement, for which I thank her.

My appreciation and gratitude extends formally to Bord na Mona, especially to Ciaran Conroy, Maire ni Domhnaill, Jerry Davey and Deirdre Hanover. Many people, both friends and colleagues, have also helped me. I would like to give a special mention to Thelma Mansfield for her belief in my ideas, to Derek Davis, Geraldine Scully, Aidan Maguire, David Kearns, Kate O'Brien, Suzanne McDougald, Patricia King, Gerry O'Neill, Bernie Walsh, Kieran Lyons, Sheamus Smith, Maureen Fitzgerald, Ita Reed Smith, Tom O'Doherty, I.C.I., Carl Barnes, Dominick Murphy, Martin Brady, Louise O'Neill, Carol O'Neill and Robin Culleton. If I have inadvertently forgotten other help given to me on this project, I offer my sincere apologies.